Parenting in a
TECH WORLD

WHAT PEOPLE ARE SAYING:

"Technology is the most powerful tool your child will have access to. This book is a great investment in yourself, your child and their future."
— *Blake Canterbury, Founder of Purposity.com, Entrepreneur, Speaker*

"I was very blessed to have an amazing Mom and Dad. I learned so much from them and have benefited from their wisdom countless times. And yet, there was one area where they couldn't help Wendy and me very much — how to parent in a high-tech world. It's why Titania and Matt's book is a gift to all of us parents. We don't have to parent out of fear. We don't have to put our heads in the sand and pretend social media doesn't exist. And most of all, we can win the technology battle. Yes, you can lead your kids through it well. This is the parenting book you've been waiting on and you'll be better because of it. And so will your kids."
— *Jeff Henderson, Lead Pastor of Gwinnett Church, Author of Know What You're FOR: A Growth Strategy for Work, An Even Better Strategy for Life*

"Titania Jordan and Matt McKee have written what most parents of teens and tweens want: A complete and straightforward book on how and why to best manage their child's digital activity. Regardless of your technical skills, you'll find this book as a critical guide to keep your family safe online — without having to pull the plug on the good that technology can also bring to your kids."
— *Stephen J. Smith, Author of Social Media & the Adolescent Digital Tribe and President of A Wired Family*

"*Parenting in a Tech World* is a parenting resource based on positive psychology using technology to encourage family bonding and healthy interaction. Highlighted are the positive opportunities technology offers to help children learn and develop the skills to prosper and stay safe as they engage the wider world around them. Parents are given straightforward knowledge, strategies, and advice on how to use technology to develop positive relationships with their children and how to keep them safe."
— *Thomas K. Pedigo., Ed.D., ABMP, Licensed Psychologist, Board Certified Medical Psychologist, Co-Founder of Esteem Therapeutics*

"Titania Jordan and Matt McKee have created something truly wonderful. The conversation around parenting, kids, and tech isn't always easy, but it's also not going away anytime soon. They've woven together an incredible and practical guide for how to dive into some of the most scary conversations and come out on the other side."
— *Jelani Memory, Founder & CEO of A Kids Book About*

"Raising children in today's world filled with technology is no easy task. We are the first generation of parents that has to raise children in both the physical and virtual worlds at the same time. Oftentimes, parents are intimidated by moderating their children's technology use; *Parenting in a Tech World* is an approachable guide for parents that provides direction on how to get the conversation started with their children to raise successful children in a challenging environment."
— *Ben Halpert, Founder & President of Savvy Cyber Kids*

Parenting in a Tech World:
A Handbook for Raising Kids in the Digital Age

Copyright ©2020 by Titania Jordan, Matt McKee, and Bark Technologies, Inc.

IRL Publishing
3423 Piedmont Road NE Suite 360
Atlanta, GA 30305

Cover design by Sean Chancey

ISBN: 978-0-578-73315-9 (hardcover)

Printed in the United States of America
First Edition: October 2020

1 2 3 4 5 6 7 8 9 10

Dedications

Titania Jordan

This book is dedicated to the awesome team at Bark, who works hard 24/7/365 to educate, empower, and protect families. This book is also dedicated to my family, whose unconditional love and unwavering support carries me through the highest of highs and the lowest of lows. Finally, but foremost, this book is dedicated to God — who continues to open doors where I only see walls.

Matt McKee

I dedicate this book to my wife Jessica and my two sons Patriot and Azlan. Without them this book about family would not mean much.

Acknowledgements

Behind every work of passion, there are a multitude of people and experiences that shape the work. We (Titania and Matt) will attempt to thank a few key people who helped bring this work to life.

We owe a big "Thank you" to Jennifer Wilder — without whom this book would still be a notes file on our laptops. Jennifer made sense of our words, brought thoughts together, and shaped this book into a parenting guide that's useful and makes sense. Thanks, Jen!

To the team at Bark and our extraordinary leader, Brian Bason, we thank you for believing that families can have a healthy relationship with technology. Thank you for the passion and countless hours you put into helping keep kids safe online. You inspire us, and lead us to be better stewards of the power of technology.

You can't have a book in the modern age without beautiful resources, so we'd like to thank MB Bell, Gabrielle Parris, Uduak Ita, and Sean Chancey for their incredible design skills — not only in this book but everywhere you encounter the Bark brand online and in real life.

Additionally, we would like to thank Haley Zapal, Dan Grammer, Jodie Sherril, Krista Smith, Leslie Rogers, Jasmine Willman, Brynn-Marie Kloser, and Jordan Bissell for staying up-to-date on the latest trends, demonstrating unparalleled dedication to the crafts of writing and community building, and helping to shape this book.

Writing a book would mean nothing if nobody were to read it, and that would be a huge bummer. We'd like to thank Adina Kalish, Justin Hackney, and Caroline Scruggs for helping us share this labor of love with the world. We have learned so much from other parents, particularly in the Parenting in a Tech World Facebook group community. Thank you to every member for engaging, building each other up, sharing information, and providing a safe place to gain confidence and wisdom about how to raise our children to use technology in healthy ways.

Though there are too many to list by name — invariably someone would be left out — we want to thank the countless experts and leaders who have shared their knowledge with us graciously and generously. Experts who have invested time and energy into helping us guide you — the parent, the reader — toward safety online. They have shared their ideas, opinions, best practices, first-hand experiences, research, and passion with us, and we are eternally grateful.

Throughout my (Titania) career in tech, I have grown acutely aware of its sheer power. As I simultaneously became addicted to social media and a mother in the span of just a few short years, I realized how necessary it was going to be for me to play a part in cultivating digital citizenship in my family. This sparked a passion that would ultimately lead me to help equip families all across the world with the information and tools needed to maintain a healthy relationship with technology. Without the support of my family — and the "training ground" for kids and tech it has provided — I wouldn't have found this calling.

Over my lifetime I (Matt) have been around incredible leaders, parents, and role models. Having access to them so that I could ask them questions and learn from them is more valuable than I will ever really know. Having grown up with two parents who are still living and still married to each other today is also invaluable. I am not sure how I picked the long straw but I am grateful. I can tell you that I am not the best parent in the world or even the world's greatest dad, but what I have learned over the years I will continue to share. I hope you find this useful, and if nothing else it might help you and your family build a better relationship.

CONTENTS

What People Are Saying:...ii

Introduction 1

Define the Win 7

Win the War, Not Every Battle...15

Where is Tech Today?...21

Learning Technology & Social Media 29

Right Questions to Ask..39

Wrong Questions To Ask 51

Conversations & Modeling..55

Creation vs. Consumption...61

Moving From Control To Influence 69

The Tech Spectrum 81

Tired of Keeping Up 97

Passwords Are Doorways...107

The New + What To Do..113

It Takes A Village 123

Good Digital Citizen 135

Be On The Lookout 141

Help Me, I Don't "Do" Tech 149

The Data...155

Conclusion 161

CHAPTER 1

INTRODUCTION

Let's start with our **why.** Having worked at the intersection of parenting and tech for the past two decades, we see the current state of parenting in a world that has never existed before, and how much pain, confusion, and frustration exists. Also, being the eternal optimists we are, we also see the opportunity that exists for education and support for society as a whole. And we have high hopes that, if followed, the steps outlined in this book will positively change the trajectory of our most vulnerable population. Since time is of the essence, let's waste none of yours.

We intend to give hope instead of fear

Will we be talking about hard, sometimes triggering issues? Absolutely. Will addressing the elephants in the room make them seem a lot smaller and less scary? Definitely.

We include action steps along the way

As a practice, we don't like to present problems without offering solutions. For every tough issue we outline, we'll give you the best next steps to help you in this parenting tech journey.

We provide resources to help when you don't know what to do

Do we know everything there is to know about parenting and tech? Definitely not. That's why we enlist the help of a variety of sites and experts to give you the best, most up-to-date insights for how to do this thing called "parenting in a tech world" well.

We've built a community to support you when something happens

How many times have you heard the phrase "it takes a village" and kind of rolled your eyes until it hit you one day that it's so very true? We have that village for you — both in a closed Facebook group called Parenting in a Tech World[1] as well as through the Bark app available for both iOS[2] and Android devices.

Here's why we care so much about this topic...

Afraid, ignorant, overwhelmed... or all of the above

Most parents we know feel one of three ways about technology when it comes to their children. They're afraid of technology and the damage it could cause. They're ignorant of technology and don't know what it can do or what they can do about it. Or, they're overwhelmed and don't know where to start with technology and all of its small nuances, settings, or features that could lead their child into scary territory. Whichever it is — feeling afraid, ignorant, or overwhelmed — almost all parents we know feel like they're always behind. Even if they have the latest gadgets and software, they live in uncertainty — fearing that the next technological gizmo or software update will make them irrelevant as parents.

Irrelevance is scary

Feeling like you're irrelevant as a parent is a strong feeling. It's not just a feeling of being uncool or left out — no one wants to be the uncool parent.

---

1   https://www.facebook.com/groups/parentinggeeks/

2   https://apps.apple.com/us/app/bark-parental-controls/id1477619146

The more painful part of irrelevance, however, is that your relationship with your children seems stripped of purpose. Being irrelevant to your children means being unable to influence or guide them. And that's scary. We know, because we've felt that way sometimes.

Dad, I don't want other kids to see what I've seen

The events that led to my (Matt) son saying, "Dad, I don't want other kids to see what I've seen," started when my oldest son was 9 years old.

While at a friend's house, my son and his friends found a new piece of technology to explore — an iPad©. They started playing, exploring, searching, and eventually, their curiosity led them to content that no 9-year-old should see. Around the same time, I started to notice some things. My son's behavior changed. He went from being open to closing himself off, and an indiscernible mood seemed to settle over him. My dad-radar went off, and I knew there was something wrong.

I needed to know what was happening, so I started by asking him a question. I didn't want to ask him something that would make him defensive, like, "What's wrong with you?" I didn't want him to shut down and shut me out. I wanted him to open up so that I could find out what was going on in his world.

I asked, "What is the most interesting thing you've seen recently?" The answer he gave shocked me and broke my heart.

Today, adult content doesn't stay hidden

In time, through more conversation, I discovered that it wasn't just one image or one occasion that something like this had happened. There were multiple times when he, either through friends or online predators, was exposed to adult content. It seemed like my son was living in a world that I didn't know. I thought I knew everything that my 9-year-old was doing in his life. I came to find out that I was very wrong.

Before we tell you the rest of the story about what happened with Matt's son, let's talk about adult content. It's likely a reason you picked up this book, and it's the type of content that scares most parents — for good reason. Pornography addiction is a growing and prevalent problem in our world. Developmental experts are now saying that an entire generation of young men may be permanently sexually damaged by their constant exposure to it,[3] and girls are equally damaged and victimized.[4] Most experts claim the driving force of this generational damage is a shift — empowered by mobile technology — toward constant, unfettered access and availability.

When I grew up, mature content was more easily limited by physical and financial barriers. When I was exposed to it, it was contained in a physical place (a magazine) that was hidden in a physical location (a family member's house). I had limited access to that location and no ability to purchase a similar magazine for myself. Today, adult content doesn't stay hidden under the bed at an uncle's house across town. It can be accessed from any innocuous-seeming device with an internet connection — at a friend's house, on the bus, in your living room, or in the back of your car. The content that exists today is also more extreme, more addicting, and contains not just nudity or sexual content, but strong themes of violence, rape, misogyny, and torture.

If you think too much about the easy availability of adult content, you could be paralyzed with fear. Titania and I know that feeling.

In the moment when I discovered what my son had been exposed to, I felt irrelevant. I felt like a failure. I wanted to be a good influence on my son and to shape his view of the world in a positive way, and yet, at a vulnerable time

---

3   http://time.com/4277510/porn-and-the-threat-to-virility/

4   http://time.com/4277523/girls-sex-women-porn/

in his development, he was victimized. Not long after that, I listened to my 9-year-old son tell me, "Dad, I don't know if I can handle this anymore."

As a parent, that made me angry — not because I thought my son was bad, but because I could see how he had been victimized by those who had taken advantage of his simple curiosity. I was angry because I want my children to be curious and to explore, but I also want them to be safe.

A problem for the whole family

To address this problem, our family had to have a conversation and go on a journey together — learning how to live with technology. You'll discover, as we did, that access to mature, sexual content is only a small part of a huge problem that we all face.

In the process, we learned some things about technology, but we learned more about ourselves. We learned that all of us were addicted to technology. It was hard to put down devices and look at each other. It was hard to disconnect from the internet and talk to each other. *This wasn't a 9-year-old's problem. It was a problem for our entire family.* And we dealt with it as a family. We all got involved and discussed the expectations, the purpose of, and the use of technology as a part of our family. That discussion went far beyond what type of content a child might be able to stumble across, and it led us to realize that we all needed to change the way we used technology. We needed to put limits on what we did in our home. When, where, and for how long we used devices — it all needed to change.

From victim to advocate

More importantly to me, however, was how our family's journey led my son from being victimized to being active in helping others avoid what happened to him. His words to me, "Dad, I don't want other kids to see what I've seen," led him to become an advocate for other children. It eventually led to a meeting with the technology director at his school, where he delivered a device to help filter content and to help keep children at his school safe.

There is hope

I share this story about my family because I imagine that, more than likely, if you are picking up this book, something bad has already happened. If so, you're in the same place I was.

I'm here to tell you that there is hope. Nothing is broken that can't be fixed. My son's story — my family's story — is here to tell you that you and your family members don't have to be victims. Taking control of our family's technology and refocusing our family on relationships was something we desperately needed, but we might never have done it had I not discovered what had happened to my son. What was broken about our family wasn't that my son saw some adult content. That was a warning sign. What was broken about us was our addiction to technology.

I thought the worst thing that could've happened was my son's exposure to adult content, but I found out that wasn't true. The worst thing that could have happened was if our family had stayed the same — addicted to technology, consumed by gadgets, and isolated from each other in our own home.

The world has always been a dangerous place for children. There has never been a time when families have been immune from or unable to be touched by any manner of danger. Our family realized that the same thing that sustained families generations ago through challenges and difficulty is still available. Relationships, conversation, love, guidance, learning, and forgiveness are tools that can both protect your family from such dangers and help your family recover when — despite your best plans and practices — something bad slips through or is stumbled upon out in the world.

CHAPTER 2

DEFINE THE WIN

When I (Matt) was a kid, our family would criss-cross central Kentucky visiting family during the holidays. The central location, or "home base," was my grandmother's house, and we were all expected to gather there to celebrate Christmas. Some of the smaller, individual families also held their own Christmas gatherings in their own homes.

Night after night, centered around the Christmas holiday, my family would travel back and forth between Christmas parties. That's what it felt like to me — a series of Christmas parties, each with their own energy, their own unique foods and treats, and their own unique memories. Some of my most vivid and enjoyable memories were made during this seasonal pilgrimage.

At the time, I didn't realize I was participating in a tradition. In fact, I didn't realize that until I was older, able to make the choice — or not — of returning to grandmother's. When I realized there was a choice, I also realized that there wasn't a choice because I *wanted* to return home. That's what Christmas was to me, bouncing from family Christmas party to family Christmas party sharing stories with others and eating really amazing food. The attraction to return was greater than any attraction to "do my own thing" at Christmas.

This Christmas tradition instilled in me the desire and the importance of returning home. It cemented the truth in my heart that I could always come home, no matter what — I'd always have something to return to. There's tremendous safety and confidence in that realization. Not only are these blood family, they're *my people* — cut from the same cloth, sharing many similar memories and values, and supporting each other through thick and thin, happiness and grief, gain and loss.

As an adult with my own wife and children, this time with family — among other experiences my parents provided for me — gave me an understanding of what launching successfully looks like. Now, *launching* may not be a typical word used for raising a child, but essentially, launching an adult into the world is our main responsibility as parents. And we want to make that launching process one that contains the common thread of family as the safe place. Family is what our kids can rely on at the ages of 5, 10, 18, 35, and beyond.

Establishing the fact that family is the safe place includes establishing that within the context of family is where fears and challenges are discussed — including technology. And because of the bonds created through traditions or consistent activities and events, we don't have to fear tech — we don't have to hide it or hide from it. For all the good things technology provides families and businesses and communities, we can also discuss and illuminate its challenges and less-than-wholesome uses as a family. Family must be the safe place where we discuss, learn, and experience healthy technology.

What do you really want to happen in your family?

Today's technology is expansive and encompassing, and it often feels overwhelming to think about every way and every access point we have of finding information and entertainment across online spaces. Often, we get so caught up in the pace of life that it's difficult to pinpoint what makes something go right (like raising a child with healthy boundaries) and what makes something go wrong (like parenting a child with an internet addiction). Many of us live in our heads and spend little time articulating, specifically, what it is that we want our kids to learn and live out when they leave our homes for college or the workforce.

You'd think that with all of today's advancements and discoveries in technology, science, human behavior, work systems, and life automation, we'd have some free time to stay present, be involved, intentionally connect, and keep up with all that our kids are doing — online and at school. But according to Parkinson's Law, work expands to the amount of time available to complete it. Even the automation of housework (efficient washers, dryers, and robot vacuums) has allowed us to do even more types of cleaning methods (like reorganizing and redecorating) thus filling up the free time we gained by the automation of other things. As the pace gets faster, and more work is produced, it's easy to get caught up in day-to-day responsibilities so much so that you lose track of what you really want to happen in your family.

There are things that we can do, though it will require the merciless carving-out of hours to make a plan — a plan for the growth and health of your family unit and your children.

Let's stretch our view of parenting children, and think of it in terms of planning a celebration. Celebrations are specific. They require the coordination of resources toward an end goal. There's a specific audience in mind, and a specific focus is accentuated. Parenting is specific to your children. It requires the coordination of resources. Society is the audience, and the focus is on raising them to be valuable members of it.
If a celebration starts with a plan, timeline, and a budget, why can't parenting incorporate some of the same tactics? No father or mother plans to be uninvolved and uninformed — no one sets out to fail. In fact, we'd

probably find most parents want to be involved, they want to teach their children meaningful things, and they want their children to succeed. So why do so many of us fail at getting specific about what we want our children to learn and experience before they leave our homes? Why not make a plan for the major milestones in their first 18 years, and write it down? The reason why we don't, and the reason why we haven't, is because we're filling our time with more work, more tasks, more responsibilities. That's why you must *mercilessly* carve out time to create an endgoal.

From technology to social responsibility to spirituality to finance to basic life skills, writing down what you want your kids to learn or experience through their adolescent years is a good starting place as you begin to intentionally prepare them for adulthood.

Let's start with the destination, and let's think primarily in terms of technology and the role it plays in our lives — bearing in mind that technology and its role will likely change dramatically over the span of 18 years.

Mapping the route

Let's determine the destination by answering this question: What is the relationship you'd like your child to have with you and with technology by the time they turn 18 years old?

There could be a number of things you'd like your children to do, say, feel, and believe in the 18 years you have of rearing them under your roof. Maybe you've seen these popular home decor items (or at least a Pinterest version) — distressed wood signs that say something like "House Rules" or "In This House..." followed by a list of phrases or characteristics. One such home decor sign reads:

In our home . . .

We do sharing

We do laughter

We do mistakes

We do real

We sometimes do silly

We do our best

We do fun

We do I'm sorrys

We do hugs

We do family

We do kindness

We do love

These types of signs are meant to be a reminder for family members about what it means to carry their last name. It's a manifesto of intentions and values your family strives toward, like being:

- Helpful
- Trustworthy
- Kind
- Resourceful
- Respectful
- Peaceful
- Confident
- Mindful
- Compassionate
- Generous
- Hopeful
- Creative

Now that you've seen two sample lists, think forward in time. Picture your son or daughter as they turn 18. You're commissioning a gift for them from a local maker, and the maker asks you to describe your child to them. What are some characteristics you'd like to use to describe your child at the age of 18? Personalize their list by including their name: [Name] is confident and self-assured.

Once you've created the list, read over it a time or two. Did you capture all the descriptive words you want to speak of your future 18-year-old? If you feel your list is complete, think about using these words in a narrative way — a story about your child. Sure, we know most of you aren't writers. But we believe that anyone is able to think about scenarios their child might experience while utilizing these characteristics, and then write down those thoughts. This exercise helps to form a visual image of what your child's characteristics will look like in real life.

For the sample list above, the narrative could be something like this:

Ethan was playing in the front yard with his sister Avery when he noticed a soggy newspaper clogging the drain along the curb of his street. As Ethan picked up the paper and deposited it into a nearby garbage can (Respectful), he heard his neighbor Mrs. Sams calling for her dog. He asked Mrs. Sams if he could help (helpful), and she asked him to go into her house and turn off her stove (trustworthy) and get some treats for the dog when it returned.

Knowing that searching and calling for a dog was a strenuous use of the voice, Ethan also filled a cup of water for Mrs. Sams and took it to her (mindful). When Ethan returned to Mrs. Sams with the water, he said: "You're probably so worried about your pup (compassionate). We're going to do what we can to find him (hopeful/peaceful)." Ethan asked Mrs. Sams for a picture of the dog, he added the picture to his phone, and he posted a missing dog announcement to neighborhood apps, and to his community's Facebook page (resourceful).

As more people joined the search for Mrs. Sams' dog, Ethan decided it would be a good idea to create a flyer (creativity) that searchers could pass around neighborhoods and post on telephone poles. After printing off several copies, Ethan distributed the flyers to other neighbors who were searching (confidence). He then jumped in his car, drove to the corner store, and bought a case of bottled water for the search party (generous).

As Ethan turned his car into his neighborhood, he saw a group of people huddled together on the sidewalk. Nearly everyone was stooped over, some were laughing, others high-fiving, as they surrounded Mrs. Sams and her dog. The search was a success, and Ethan stopped the car and began handing out celebratory bottles of water to his neighbors.

It's fine if you think this is a corny idea. But didn't reading the story provide an even more robust picture of *who* Ethan is?

Creating a narrative like this helps to keep the goal in mind. If it's easier, think of writing a sentence about your child around each descriptive word. That way there isn't any pressure to create a cohesive story.

For example, I (Titania) wrote this narrative about my son, Jackson:

The goal is that when my only son no longer lives under our roof, he still wants to come back, and often. I want him to look forward to the holidays and not dread them.

I want him to be able to share his hopes, dreams, fears, wins, mistakes, and everything in between with me — knowing that I will not judge him and that my love for him is unconditional.

I want Jackson to grow up to be a kind and resilient man, who considers the feelings of others and the long-term implications of both his interpersonal and digital actions.

I hope that he doesn't succumb to a pornography or gaming addiction. I hope that he's intuitive enough to recognize when he has taken a misstep, and can humbly own it and take necessary actions to remedy it.

I hope that he uses his gifts to bring glory to his Creator, and that he shines as a light in this world. (Jackson, if you are reading this: Hi! And I love you.)

Now, the sometimes-not-easy part is working backward from this endgoal to determine how I conduct myself, what I expose my child to, and how we maintain our parent-child bond through adolescence in order to reach this picture.

There isn't a manual for every conversation, every situation, every mistake or triumph that you're going to encounter. But something we believe in is keeping the endgoal in mind. Reread your list of descriptive words. Read the narrative you wrote of your child every day. Take each word and decide when to have a discussion about what each word means and why it's important to your family.

CHAPTER 3

WIN THE WAR, NOT EVERY BATTLE

We can all agree that these are very different times from when we were kids. And in turn, our childhoods were very different from our parents'. Though tech advancements didn't seem as fast-paced as they are today, we see that we went from LPs to MP3s in our childhood. We went from Atari to Wii; from handheld football games to Nintendo Game Boys. There was no social element to our entertainment, other than the show recaps on the swingset at school the next day at recess. The only dangers our parents suspected from this entertainment were wasted time, weary eyes, and inactivity — all serious things at the time.

Each generation has had its serious thing, its battles that had to be fought. Our early ancestors were nomads who braved making homesteads in deserts, amid harsh conditions. They had to save their children from poisonous insects, wild beasts, and deadly plants. Their weapons were primitive and their knowledge was limited — lessons were usually passed down through storytelling. Food was hunted or gathered which brought its own dangers — of exposure to the elements, other hunting tribes, and wild animals. Every day was a risk and a test of survival.

As time passed and more civilized homesteads emerged, parents kept their children safe from plagues that swept through communities and risked their own health to get treatment and medical supplies. They limited activities or forced activities depending on the kind of ailment or disease their child had contracted. They provided for their children, they worried, and they battled with their children to take medicine or the newest treatments.

A battle currently emerging around the world is one against COVID-19, a coronavirus that is spreading rapidly and killing thousands. As we live through what the World Health Organization has classified as a pandemic, schools are moving to online classes, restaurants are closing their dining rooms, and grocery store shelves are emptied nightly by concerned citizens bracing for a long-haul of time in quarantine. And with kids at home during the quarantine, parents are fighting to balance screen time with learning and activity in new ways — especially as they themselves are dealing with business closures, working from home, and potential loss of income.

There are other battles that parents have fought over the years too — like addictions. These are addictions to things that were initially created for good but are being used beyond what they were originally intended for. Nearly every generation has been challenged with creating boundaries or safeguards or rules around something that was designed to be beneficial, but easily becomes harmful if it's used outside of the way it was intended.

For example, the use of drugs dates back to the earliest days of civilization because they were used in religious ceremonies (mushrooms), to aid the sick (opium), and in socially acceptable stress-relieving forms (alcohol, tobacco, and marijuana).

As our ancestors created more potent strains and faster ways to produce different drugs, the abuse of drugs began, and sadly, that abuse has continued to this day. The battles over effective treatments for addictions and the understanding of how addictions work have been fought for decades, even centuries. Then, in the mid-20th century researchers discovered a "pleasure center" in our brains. A pleasure center that, when activated, creates addictive bonds between our brains and our use of stimulants.

 The so-called 'pleasure center' of the brain was co-discovered in 1954 by James Olds, who was an American psychologist, and Peter Milner while he was a postdoctoral fellow at McGill University. Olds and Milner stumbled on the pleasure center after they implanted electrodes into the septal area of the rat and found that rats became addicted to pushing a lever that was stimulating the nucleus accumbens (NAcc).[5]

Addictive substances like alcohol, drugs, food, and tobacco trigger the release of dopamine in the *nucleus accumbens* — also known as one of the brain's reward centers. A Google search of the keywords "screen time" and "nucleus accumbens" brings up article after article and study after study of links between social media and gaming. Addictions are formed during gaming or when we're on social media because both avenues cause dopamine to be released in this reward, or pleasure, center. To put it bluntly: social media and gaming are drugs to our brains.

To put it another way, one of this generation's battles against addiction comes in the form of tech.

5   https://www.psychologytoday.com/us/blog/the-athletes-way/201405/the-neuroscience-pleasure-and-addiction

Authors Frances E. Jensen, M.D., and Amy Ellis Nutt say it best in their book, *The Teenage Brain (A Neuroscientist's Survival Guide to Raising Adolescents and Young Adults)*: "The cascade of neuroprocesses that kicks off the brain's reward circuitry, and the rush of the pleasure chemical dopamine, can be triggered just as easily by the release of the latest iPhone as by alcohol, pot, sex, or a fast car."

Reframe the problem

Because of my (Titania) passion for this subject — keeping kids safer online — reading psychology journals, parenting forums, and numerous books on the subject is part of my job. With all this information processing through my brain, a light bulb went off for me one time when I became frustrated with my son, Jackson, about him not responding to me.

For the longest time, I'd blow my lid over the fact that when Jackson's face was in front of a screen, he wouldn't do what I said, when I said it, like... right away. I saw it as an act of defiance. After many years of yelling and tears, one day, I gained a key insight and reframed the problem. How could I expect my son to even hear what I was saying when the lights and sounds and movement in front of his eyeballs were stimulating the pleasure centers of his brain?[6]

I explained to Jackson that when he didn't respond to me, it appeared he was no longer in control of his body. And what does a child want? Control. I had his ear. I told him that when he's in front of the TV, or iPad, or PS4, or anything else with a screen, the part of his brain that loves and craves sweets lights up, causing the stimulus to take over. I asked him who was in charge — the screen, or him? Removing me as the "bad guy" and refocusing the problem on tech enabled us to band together to solve the problem.

---

6   https://www.psychologytoday.com/us/blog/the-athletes-way/201405/the-neuroscience-pleasure-
     and-addiction

The important thing to remember as you set out to guide your child away from the entrapment that technology can bring is that this is all a long-term play. This is a long-term war, and there are battles that will be played along the way. One battle might be over how your son or daughter isn't being responsible. Another battle might be over honesty. And another battle might be over acceptable ways to use technology in your home.

There are smaller battles you might not always fight — like a battle over doing the dishes one night or which restaurant to pick for dinner. These are inconsequential to the ultimate goal of raising a healthy adult.

The small battles won't impact whether or not your adult kids will return for Thanksgiving dinner. It's the big battles — honesty, being a good friend, being responsible, doing their best, and managing technology well, etc. — where the anchors of relationships are fixed. That's where trust is built, ideas are shared, and bonds are formed. It's in the more difficult battles where things hang in the balance — things like the ability to make good decisions, the ability to exercise self-control, the ability to practice patience, the ability to foresee potential problems.

These types of battles require intention, maybe research, definitely patience — boatloads of patience — empathy, sometimes grace, and sometimes mercy. These battles are your opportunity to show your child how to handle problems, find solutions, collaborate, and resolve conflict. We are *positive* (sarcasm font) you'll remember what an opportunity you have as you're in the midst of an argument about a cellphone that was snuck into a bedroom in order to text a classmate at 1 a.m.

Remember, you're in this for the long haul — and at times it's going to be grueling. You'll feel like battles are raging every day. You'll feel tired, disappointed, spent, and hopeless. But you won't be for long. You may have to dig really deep some days, but you'll have more to give because this is the most important role you'll ever have in your life. Fight the appropriate battles well, because you want your adult kids to come home for Thanksgiving dinner.

CHAPTER 4

WHERE IS TECH TODAY?

We called my (Matt) favorite uncle, Uncle Bobo, or sometimes just Bobo. He was my favorite because he was so fun to be around — I'd never know if he was telling the truth or making things up. He'd tease me — mercilessly, sometimes — and I'd eat up the attention. So when he sat me down to share a secret with me, I was glued to his every word:

"Matthew, every night I meet up with Superman and we fly all over the area, even out over the lake," Uncle Bobo said.

My eyes grew wide and my mouth slacked. Superman was my absolute favorite superhero! I couldn't miss the chance to meet him and fly with him!

"How?" I asked, excitedly. "Can I fly with you and Superman tonight?"

Uncle Bobo went on to explain the intricate details of why I couldn't fly with him and Superman that night. The most important being that I didn't have the right shoes.

"In order to fly with us, you have to have a pair of red, white, and blue Nike®

shoes," Uncle Bobo explained as he looked into my expectant eyes.

Though my heart sunk, and I was sad I couldn't go this time, I was hopeful that with the right gear — and for our purposes in this book, the right tech — I'd be flying with Uncle Bobo and Superman the next time I came to visit.

For months, I begged my parents for red, white, and blue Nikes. I became a broken record, repeating my request at even the slightest mention of shopping — even grocery store shopping.

So when I finally received the red, white, and blue Nike shoes, I was overjoyed to think about how much fun I'd have flying with Uncle Bobo and Superman. At the next family gathering, I proudly presented my new shoes to Uncle Bobo. His enthusiasm to see my flying shoes faded as he inspected the tongue of the shoe.

"Oh, no, Matthew," he said solemnly. "The tongue is supposed to be red. These won't work to fly in."

I stared at my cool new shoes and my excitement evaporated. I wouldn't be able to fly with Uncle Bobo and Superman.

But then, my spirits picked up as I realized it was still possible for my dream to come true. I just needed the right tech — the shoes with the red tongue. Though I looked for months, I never did find the right shoes for flying *with* Superman, but I continued to hold out hope that one day I'd be able to fly *like* Superman.

That experience with Uncle Bobo and the red, white, and blue Nike shoes nurtured a natural curiosity in me. It helped me to understand hope and perseverance in a new way. Even today, I'm hopeful to get my pilot's license so that I can fly, and when I do, I'll be wearing red, white, and blue Nikes.

Remember the time...

Technology has changed a lot over time and, as it changed, we changed with it. We're different from our parents partly because of the effects of technology, and the same is true for our children.

Adults and children perceive time differently. The years just seem to go by more quickly to us, don't they? To children, however, time doesn't move at all or seems to crawl imperceptibly. We feel rushed and anxious, while they feel trapped and bored. We lean back, wanting to slow down because we feel we're speeding along faster and faster, while they lean forward, longing to push ahead into a future that can't get here fast enough.

If you have children, all it takes is looking back at your first pictures of them for you to realize how quickly they grow and how quickly time seems to be passing. We think to ourselves, "Where did that time go?" Years seem to pass like weeks or days. But to your children, those years took... years! And if you ask them about it, the weeks took years too! Time moves slowly from their perspective.

Part of the reason for this is that, to a 10-year-old, one year is 10% of their life, which is a lot when compared to an adult. To a 40-year-old, one year is 2.5% of their life. Also, children are gaining many new experiences and new ideas that are leaving lasting impressions that they'll carry with them for the rest of their lives. For adults, we experience less of these new things because of the years we've lived. This makes it seem like childhood lasted longer than it did.[7]

Because last year can feel just like last week to us, we make two key mistakes when we think about our children:

---

7   https://www.nbcnews.com/better/health/why-our-sense-time-speeds-we-age-how-slow-it-ncna936351

- **We think our children are just like we were.**
- **We think they're growing up like we grew up.**

In our minds, we think we aren't that different from our children. Because our younger selves seem so close in our memories, we think that we know what our children are like because we know what we were like. However, they're very different from us because the world they were born into is so very different from the world we were born into.

Here's some perspective for you. Start by thinking of your child's birthdate. Got that date fixed in your mind? Below, we've listed some events and dates. Your job is to think one of two words after each date: "before" if your child was born before the date, or "after" if your child was born after the date.

- The first televised advertisement featuring the first iPhone® was broadcast during the 79th Academy Awards in February of 2007. To remind you how long ago that was, *Happy Feet, Cars,* and *Monster House* were nominated for Best Animated Feature. (*Cars* should have won.) *An Inconvenient Truth* won Best Documentary and *The Departed* won Best Picture.
- The first iPhones were sold on June 29, 2007.[8]
- The Apple App Store debuted on July 10, 2008.
- *Angry Birds* was originally released for Apple iOS in December of 2009.

How many times did you think "before"? We're guessing not very many. We don't know when you're reading this book, but any child younger than 12 has never lived in a world that didn't have iPhones in it. Just think for a minute about life in the pre-iPhone days.

Before that iconic, introductory advertisement during the Academy Awards, most people saw no need for a "smart" phone. Sure, business professionals

---

8   http://www.wired.com/2009/06/dayintech_0629/

had Blackberry® phones but, for average people, Blackberrys were not seen as something they needed. But, when iPhone showed up on television screens in family homes and said "Hello," the way we thought about phones began to change.

Think of all the things you do with your phone that you used to do in other ways. Your phone is probably within reach as you read this book — or you're actually reading this book on your phone. Before your children were born, many of the tasks you just thought of would require getting up, perhaps leaving the house, or using multiple forms of technology. Now, the power to do all of those things is right beside you. And your children have never known anything different.

Technology has radically changed our world, and it won't stop changing it. Technology has changed the way we think, the way we learn, the way we work, and the way we socialize. Your children don't do any of those things in the same way that you did. But that doesn't mean you can't communicate with them effectively. It doesn't mean technology wins. In fact, parents win. Why? Because parents can do something that technology can't. As a parent, you can have a relationship with your children in a way that technology can't — no matter how much it progresses.

Parents and children still form memories around real things in their lives. No one says, "Remember that time I posted that picture on Facebook?" Memories are built around real events with real people in the real world, things like:

- The first concert you went to
- Your 16th birthday
- Your high school graduation
- A family vacation to the beach

Even when we do remember an event that involves technology, we remember it because of the relationships involved, not because of the technology itself.

- That photo on Facebook that got a bunch of great comments? We remember the moment the photo was taken, the other people in the photo, the person who took the photo, and the people who commented on it — not the phone that took it.
- That great moment your children had when playing an online game? It's their friends that they remember — not the game or the gaming system.
- The last-minute play that ended up with your team making it to the playoffs? It's the hugs and high-fives you shared with your best friends, not the TV you watched it on.

Relationships trump technology every time. Why? Because technology amplifies our longing for relationships. We just need to make sure that when our children long for relationships, they know how to have one. Our biggest opportunities with our children have nothing to do with technology. They have to do with being with them in the important moments of life and having conversations about things that matter to them.

Children aren't going to look back and say, "remember when" about technology. But they will say, "Remember when you were there for me?" "Remember when we did that thing together?" "Remember when you helped me not to be scared?" "Remember when you encouraged me after I failed?" "Remember when we celebrated?"

For them to say "remember when" about you, there needs to be a "when" that you were there. As time races by you, are you making time to be present in the moments that matter for your children? We know — that sentence hit us in the gut too. Remember, you feel time passing quickly, but they feel it passing slowly. When you say — either with your words or your actions — that you don't have time for them, part of the reason they don't understand is because to them, time is slow and all they have is time.

Technology can do some amazing things for your children, and your children will use technology to do some things that will amaze you. But technology can't do for your children what you can do — have a real relationship with them.

What's happening with technology doesn't have to determine what happens in our families. There are relational and technological ways to address this problem. After all, relationships are built around conversations, and conversations start with questions. The first conversation and the first questions we need to ask are about the purpose and power of the technology that we're considering bringing into our homes and our lives. We'll discuss all of this and more in the upcoming chapters of this book.

CHAPTER 5

LEARNING TECHNOLOGY & SOCIAL MEDIA

When I (Matt) was a teenager, my best friend, Brian, was a little older than me — which meant he got his driver's license before I did. One winter night, Brian talked me into sneaking out of my house and going for a drive with him in his Camaro. Think about that: a kid new to driving, in winter conditions (read ice and snow), behind the wheel of a Camaro. And if you didn't know this already, a Camaro was a big deal type of car in my day.

So, I snuck out of my house and went to Brian's house down the street. We were careful to push the car out of the garage and down the driveway before we cranked it in the street. Camaros weren't known for being quiet — I guess no cars were at that time. So we knew we needed to be careful if we didn't want to be heard.

Once safely cranked in the street, we eased down the street until we were out of sight from our houses. For an added element of danger, this happened in winter, with snow on the ground and freezing temperatures, which meant any snow that melted during the day froze to ice in the evening. As we drove, we'd notice a tire spin, or the steering start to swerve when we hit snow or ice patches. I guess we thought it would be fun and easier to do donuts on the slick roadways. And boy, was it so much easier to spin around 360 degrees on ice than it was on pavement. What a ride!

To recap, two 16-year-old kids, new to driving, at the helm of a powerful Camaro, in the dead of night, in winter.

After our fun night out, we eased back to the house, carefully pushing the Camaro — engine off — into the driveway and into the garage. We entered the house, and there stood Brian's dad waiting for him. This was before beepers and car phones and cell phones, so there was no way to know what we were in for until we walked into Brian's house and faced his dad.

What followed was a very uncomfortable conversation about responsibilities and trust and dangers and consequences. Yep, consequences. Consequences that amounted to no car keys, no after school hangs, no weekend cruising — only homework and curfews existed in our worlds for the next few months. It was excruciating. And it was memorable. We didn't screw up in that same way ever again. (Let's be honest, that wasn't the last poor decision Brian and I made.)

Educate

It's likely that far before your child is allowed to have a cell phone or a social media account, they'll witness you using social media on your phone or online. Of course, you want to educate your kids about social media and technology in general before they are allowed to use it on a personal device. And maybe you envision that education as a major "talk" you have with your child one-on-one, similar to the talk you plan to have about the birds and the bees.

The truth is, you've been educating your child about technology and social media most of their lives — you just didn't know it. You've taken pictures of birthday parties and life milestones and posted those to social media. They've heard you tell your spouse that so-and-so commented on this or that picture. They've seen you scrolling and liking and reading posts and laughing. They've learned that social media is entertaining.

Your kids are also getting an education from their friends. Even if your child doesn't have a phone or a social media account, there's likely a child in your kid's friend group who has one or who has access to one. Maybe these kids have gathered around an older brother's phone to look at provocative pictures — either gruesome or sexual — and they've learned that social media can be used to shock and make people uncomfortable.

Kids aren't often educated about what social media's purpose is — why it's a popular tool for connecting, and how to participate in a social media community responsibly.

So, let's go there. This is going to take some effort on your part, because we want you to be educated too. For the particular social media app you're considering allowing your child to have an account with, type the following phrase into Google: "What is the purpose of [name of social media app]?" Within about a half-second, you'll find 1.7 billion results for Facebook, and about 1.6 billion results for Instagram. These results will be more than adequate for you to learn what these applications aim to contribute to the world. From the purpose statements you read, think about how you can translate that purpose into your or your child's usage of the platform. What you're doing is educating them on participating in the community versus observing the community.

Certainly, you'll want to educate your kids as best you can, and in appropriate ways, to the dangers of social media. Just as there are people in real life who wish to do harm to us — robbers, rapists, and racists — those types of people are online too. What may start out as seemingly harmless banter may grow into what's called *grooming* for sexual exploitation. A new friend asking for a few dollars to help them get dinner one night could turn into the exchange of credit card information days later to be used fraudulently.

Sadly, online predators aren't the only risks for kids on the web — they also face racism, bullying, harassment, and more. Each topic is worthy of initial and ongoing conversations with your kids. Not only are these topics complicated, but they're bigger than a kid. Like a small child walking through a crowded parking lot filled with cars, a kid's presence is bigger and safer when they're holding onto an adult's hand. Be sure to have ongoing conversations with your kids about these topics — your wisdom and your experience will be an asset as they wade through.

One of the truths that kids don't often realize is the weight of hurtful words and pictures. Words are powerful — whether they're typed or spoken. It's so simple to type a comment, but it's just as powerful (and potentially hurtful) as saying it to someone's face. Not only can it be just as hurtful, it is definitely longer lasting.

Our kids need to understand that what they post online in any forum, on any device (even those that claim posts "disappear") are permanent posts. Each post creates a unique web page for that entry. And though some posts disappear from apps like Instagram stories or Snapchat posts, those web pages still exist, and can be surfaced from online databases. If found, this could affect your child's career aspirations, their reputation, and their credibility.

In fact, have you ever heard of the Wayback Machine? The Wayback Machine is a digital archive of the World Wide Web, founded by the

Internet Archive, a nonprofit organization based in San Francisco. It allows the user to go "back in time" and see what websites looked like in the past. For folks who had blogs or Myspace pages back in the day? You might want to see what exists about you online. Also, while you're down that rabbit hole, trying Googling yourself and your significant other. We can guarantee your children will — if they haven't already. Make your online reputation and digital footprint something that won't come back to haunt you by being thoughtful about what you decide to share.

Additionally, *who* your child follows on social media is just as important to their future. Naturally, your child will want to follow their friends, and for the most part, that will probably be harmless. So, until you're given a reason to restrict which friends your kids can follow, allow them to follow their classmates and teammates. Aside from friends, you'll also want to educate your child on how to identify questionable accounts. From profile pictures to the use of hashtags, it's important to guide your children to make smart decisions about who is worth following. A general rule of thumb is that, if you don't know them in real life, you don't follow them online — even if this person claims they're friends with one of your friends.

When faced with friending someone they don't know, or when asked to type something or send a picture they don't want to send, make sure they understand that they can say "No" to anyone, and they aren't less of a friend or student or person. This is a lesson you'll have to repeat time and again. If you weren't aware, sexting is the new first base. Let that sink in for a moment. Our kids are living in a whole new world, with pressures unlike those we faced as tweens and teens.

Another part of the way kids form their identity — which includes their online identity — is through their family. In most ways, we are who we are because of the family we came from — good or bad. In the late-1990s, two psychologists developed a "Do you know?" scale[9] in order to test the hypothesis that children who know more about their family history coped better when going through life challenges than children who know little of their family history.[10]

In 2001, the assessments were conducted with dozens of families. The sessions were recorded, and the results of the research were overwhelming: The more children knew about their families and where they came from, the stronger their sense of control over their own lives, the higher their self-esteem, and the more successfully they believed their families functioned.

We believe that sharing family stories with your children gives them a foundation and a history from which they can build the life they want. Again, helping a child build a strong foundation for their identity is a lesson you'll repeat for years and decades to come.

For you, there may be other things you'd like to educate your child about before they have access to a personal device or social media account — lessons about kindness, authenticity, gossip, and modesty. Commit to an atmosphere of communication in your home so that the family learns and grows together. Don't be afraid to be vulnerable with your children and surface mistakes you've made, decisions you wish you could take back, and friendships you should have avoided. Let them know that despite appearances, mom and dad are imperfect. This simple acknowledgment can help create space for more open and honest conversations.

9   https://www.psychologytoday.com/us/blog/the-stories-our-lives/201611/the-do-you-know-20-questions-about-family-stories

10   https://www.nytimes.com/2013/03/17/fashion/the-family-stories-that-bind-us-this-life.html

Enable

One question that's often asked is, "When do I get my child a smartphone?" Though the answer will be different for every family, we know that most social media platforms don't allow user accounts for children under the age of 13. Can you or your child fudge on the birth date entered into the account? Of course, but if makers of the app think kids younger than 13 shouldn't be on their platform, maybe waiting isn't the worst idea.

Some families choose to allow basic cellphones that are used for calling and texting only. Other families jump right into the deep end of the pool and give their children a two- or three-year-old smartphone. The level of technological sophistication is up to you, though phones with more basic features are sometimes easier to monitor, and they're a great way of building trust with your child until they can advance to the next level of responsibility.

Building trust is what you're after when you enable your kids to have access to technology and social media. It's important to help them understand that they'll be given a little bit of access until they prove that they're able to handle the platforms well. You might consider a check-in every few months to evaluate whether it's time for them to have more access or more freedom. A good rule of thumb: Don't be the first to let your child have that new device or join that social media platform. But also, don't be the last, either!

Ride beside

The requirements for getting a learner's permit have changed drastically since we first learned to drive. When we were 15, we passed a written test and then spent the next year begging our parents to let us drive them to the grocery store, to church, to soccer practice, and anything else we left the house in our car to do.

These days, there is a checklist of items a student driver must complete before taking the final driver's license test. In the state of Georgia, an applicant must:[11]

- Pass the road skills test with a minimum score of 75%.
- Have a parent or guardian present.
- Pay the $32 fee for a Class D license (which is valid for eight years).
- Hold a valid learner's permit for one year and one day.
- Have a Georgia DDS certificate of attendance notarized by the school (which is valid for 30 days or valid May–August during the summer).
- Earn an alcohol and drug awareness program certificate.
- Earn a Certificate of Completion of 30-hour driver's ed course at a state-certified driving school.
- Have a driving experience Affidavit (signed by parents) which must be completed at the Department of Driver Services. It affirms the applicant has a minimum of 40 hours of driving, six of which must be at night.
- Present valid registration and insurance for the vehicle used on the road test. (The vehicle is not required to be in the applicant's name.)

These new requirements incorporate a lot of "ride beside" hours by way of driver's education teachers and the learning driver's parents. Why do you think someone learning to drive needs to spend a year having an adult riding with them everywhere they drive? Easy question, right? Because they have no experience, they aren't accustomed to checking every angle when making a turn, they don't have their reflexes tuned in to braking or accelerating, they don't know all the features of the car, and on and on. They need someone riding beside them because driving is a big responsibility, and they need guidance.

Just like driving, using technology and social media is a big responsibility. And though technology and social media aren't inherently "good" or "bad," the way that we use them can be helpful or hurtful to others (and ourselves).

---

11   https://drivesmartgeorgia.com/blog/requirements-get-georgia-drivers-license/

So what does "riding beside" look like on social media? It means starting to learn what your child's online world looks like — from top to bottom. Find out about what their friends post online, as well as the YouTube stars, influencers, meme accounts, and musicians they follow on their social media accounts. If you can, follow them from your own account, too. This way, you'll get firsthand knowledge of what they're all about, and what your kid is learning from them.

You may come across things you're not ready for you kid to see: profanity, sexual content, and more. There can be a lot to monitor, and it's hard to review every single thing they may encounter. Fortunately, you don't have to — there are time-saving tools that can help (like Bark, which we'll talk about later in this book).

Because you'll be following all of the accounts your child follows, you'll be able to ask questions to your child about what they saw. For example, if one of your child's friends posts something questionable, you can ask your child what they thought of it. This can open a dialogue around often-undiscussed topics. It will also help you gain a better idea of what kind of a friend this person is to your child.

Riding beside your child in their online world also means reviewing their content, and helping them to understand the difference between what is a helpful post that makes a contribution to a platform, and what is just "noise" on the platform. Sometimes, a post can be hurtful, either intentionally or unintentionally. Helping children develop a discernment muscle will better equip them to make their own wise decisions.

Give boundaries

The consequences you and I experienced as kids were the result of crossing boundaries and of disobeying our parents. Even if there were no specific boundaries stated about taking the car to perform donuts on ice-covered roads in the middle of the night, there were rules about telling the truth and having integrity — which both of were broken with the sneaking part. If it had been okay to joyride, then it would've been done in broad daylight for friends to see. But it was wrong, and consequences were incurred as a result of breaking boundaries.

So, why don't we still do that for our kids? Why don't we provide adequate consequences for crossing boundaries? Maybe we don't remember how our parents did it. Thinking back to our childhoods, there are probably some good tactics and some not-so-good tactics that our parents deployed over the years. Have you ever examined what worked for you and why it did so? Are there nuggets of wisdom from your parents or grandparents that you can incorporate into your own parenting?

Setting expectations, voicing boundaries, and mapping out consequences helps parents hold their children accountable when they disobey or misbehave. However, the most ineffective parenting becomes apparent when consequences aren't followed through. Consequences equal to the misdeed must be ones that we, as parents, are willing to carry out. The process of doing so has the potential to create trust, strengthen parent-child bonds, and lead to opportunities for greater responsibility.

Do children want boundaries? They will tell you no with their mouths, and yes with their behavior. Boundaries provide security and safety, something that children (and adults) crave. Boundaries also provide an "out" — whether kids will admit it or not, telling their friends that their parents "won't let them" provides a way to save face amid peer pressure. And boundaries provide a greater sense of self in children, resulting in more healthy decision-making and behavior. Boundaries are a good thing. Are they comfortable, fun, or easy? Not at all, and they aren't meant to be. Boundaries are nothing more than clear-as-crystal expectations for actions and behaviors. They provide a landscape of freedom within set borders.

CHAPTER 6

RIGHT QUESTIONS TO ASK

Many parents, us included, aren't good at asking the right kinds of questions to their children. Most of the time, when we pick up our kids from school, we ask, "How was your day?" And, predictably, most children will answer this question in the most succinct way possible. They'll either say, "fine," "good," "okay," or usually just say nothing.

It's easy to blame our kids. Sure, they could expand and tell us more, but if they're tired or frustrated, a one-word response satisfies the question. But the problem is often with the questions we're asking. As parents, we need to not settle for monotone answers often accompanied by a grunt. We need to start asking better questions — leading questions — that cause children to reflect, to think, and hopefully to answer with more than one word. We especially need to do so around technology that we are nervous about or don't quite know our way around yet. Many parents will try to start a conversation with a weak question like, "What are you doing online?" That question is rarely going to net anything other than, "Nothing."

On the flip side, don't think this means you should ask highly specific questions, either. Asking specific, pointed questions is great for testing or for police work, but it's lousy for starting conversations. Instead of asking a direct question demanding a specific answer, you need to use open-ended questions that can be answered from a wide range of a child's experiences. Asking open-ended questions will get your child to open up about what's really happening in their life, as well as what's going on in their head. The question that helped me (Matt) discover the situation with my son was an open-ended question. If I hadn't discovered what was going on as quickly as I had, much more damage could have been done to my son and my family.

Think about questions this way — they should serve two purposes: to instill confidence and to cause creativity. Author Hugh O. Stewart[12] says that, to instill confidence in the individual to whom the question is asked, you want the person you are directing the question toward to feel like their answer will make a difference or provide some valuable input. And second, you want your question to cause creativity, so the individual can use their imagination and problem-solving skills when answering it.

Here are a few guidelines for the types of questions you should ask, followed by questions that should be a part of your regular conversations.

Guidelines to get started

Don't ask about technology

You don't have to ask about technology to get answers about technology. Children don't see their digital lives as being separate from their regular lives. When you ask about them talking to their friends, they don't separate talking in-person to their friends, texting their friends, talking to their friends via in-game chat, FaceTiming their friends, or talking to their friends via social media. It's all just talking to their friends. What we think of as "real" communication and "digital" communication are all part of one

---

12   https://www.entrepreneur.com/article/320340

big, connected world to them. When you ask an open-ended question, if it relates to a part of their digital world, you'll hear about it.

Ask for their opinion or input, not facts

If you ask for a fact, once the question is answered, the conversation is over. Asking for your children's opinions leads to further discussion. You want to ask questions that show that you value what your children think. Ask questions that encourage them to evaluate their life and express an opinion, make an evaluation, or give input about it. Then you can talk about why they feel or think that way.

Listen carefully. And ask a follow-up question

Children may seem hesitant at first, but you will be surprised how quickly they will open up to you and how much they will share with you. You need to listen carefully. Listen to them and then ask a follow-up question. Follow-up questions still need to be open, but should take you deeper into your child's world. Some examples of basic follow-up questions are:

- What does that mean?
- Why would he do that?
- How does that work?

After some practice, you won't have any trouble coming up with great questions and follow-up questions to start conversations with your children, but it can be intimidating at first. We've written some questions below that we hope will provide you with some great insight and encourage great conversations for your family. Start with these questions. Then, begin editing them, changing them, and coming up with questions of your own. Oh, and be sure to put your phone away (or at least put it on silent) when engaging with them.

Questions for opening up

What have you seen recently that was really interesting?
This is a great question to get an idea of what it is like inside your child's world. What are they looking at? What are they focusing on? What concerns them? What is catching their attention? This question will let you know all of that and sometimes more. Some things will be trivial of course, but sometimes you will be shocked by their insight into the world around them.

What is the craziest thing your friends are doing right now?
When asking this question, it's important to not make it sound accusatory or negative. You want to get positive "crazy" things as well as some boundary-pushing ones. The best thing about this question is it focuses attention on their friends. Friendships are becoming more and more important to your kid — how they talk about their friends can reveal a lot. Getting to know your children's friends will show you a picture of the path your child is on. Your children won't mind telling on their friends a little bit. It makes them look good by comparison. Doing so lets them gauge your reaction to how bad something is without actually having to do it. Remember, also, that what their friends are doing now, they'll be doing soon — or may already be doing. In any case, this question gives you a window into a vital part of their world: their friends.

What is something that surprised you recently?
Again, the answers to this question could be anything: a video they saw, something a friend said, some disappointment at home or school, or a new website they discovered. Anything surprising is noteworthy in your child's world and is usually something they will want to explore again.

Can you teach me how...?
Children love to show us things. When you allow yourself to be taught by

your child, you are seeing them learn to communicate and explain things, and you are learning about areas that are important to them. Children love to show you how smart they are and they enjoy sharing things that excite them. When there is something in your life that your child is passionate about, one of the best things you can do as a parent is to ask your child to educate you about their passion. Sitting down to play Minecraft with your 8-year-old might seem painful, but it will mean the world to them and help you see if there are things you need to know. Is there an option for in-game chat with strangers? Is night mode the reason why my kid has nightmares about farming all of a sudden? You get the idea.

If you could create anything, what would it be, and why?

Tapping into a child's creativity introduces the idea of participating or contributing versus idle consumption. Asking your child to dream in this way allows them to see how they could contribute or possibly solve a problem. And this active, participatory creativity helps to fight anxiety and depression, suicidal thoughts, fear of missing out, and it nurtures confidence, self-esteem, and leadership. Technology was created to create, and it morphed into a consumption tool for the masses. Given the appropriate guidance, our kids can return to creating and contributing, and they can use technology and social media platforms to do so. What we'll find is that they can't do both at the same time — create and consume.

How much time do you want to spend on [platform]?

When is the last time you asked for your child's input on setting expectations? Maybe not ever. Or maybe you do it often. Asking for your child's input during the process of creating an expectation of behavior helps them to take ownership of the expected behavior. It also provides us parents with the ability to hold our children accountable. If your son or daughter tells you that they only want to spend two hours a week on YouTube, and they go over that, then you have a way of guiding a conversation about the time they've spent.

As you ask this question, and as you agree on the expectations, it's a good idea to write down what has been decided upon. Seeing things written down, in ink, creates a more permanent and impactful moment of agreement between you both. Given the appropriate context of the conversation, when your child sees their allowable time to spend on the platform, they may decide to spend less time. Figure out a way to explain how long two, three, or four hours of time online is — and do so in a way that makes an impact on them at their level. Two hours of YouTube is four 30-minute videos. Or, two hours is equivalent to one movie. For more hands-on or crafty kids, two hours is painting two pictures or building a treasure box or putting together a LEGO brick set.

What do you want to get out of this?

Every app development team created their product — Facebook, Twitter, Instagram, Snapchat, etc. — with a purpose. They didn't blindly start writing code to see what would happen or to see what they could create. The question of, "What do you want to get out of it?" is a nod to determining a purpose for your child's time on the platform. As you introduce your child to the idea of a purpose, you gain perspective on their motivations. This perspective will help you develop a purpose for the platform with them.

Good conversations lead to good information

Making conversation a priority in your home won't accomplish much if the conversations don't lead anywhere interesting. To help your conversations engage your children, start with the types of questions we've included here. Your goal is to make your children the stars of the conversation. Get them sharing about their world, their friends, their opinions, and their favorite things. The information you gain will be valuable in protecting your family in the realm of technology, but it won't be nearly as valuable as the growing strength of your relationship with your children.

Our children are learning more than we ever have and learning it faster (and earlier) than we ever did. Technology is a huge part of that. Right now, the best experiences with technology for our families are when we are sitting with our kids learning from them after asking a "Can you teach me..." kind of question. Those moments are precious, and you can have those kinds of moments with your children too. But they'll never come if you don't make time for conversation and learn to ask the right questions.

From relational solutions to technical solutions

The best solutions for helping your children with technology are the ones we have just talked about — the relational solutions. However, there are many technical solutions that we outline in this book that can help keep your children safer online. Although technical solutions might involve buttons, settings, passwords, and timers, don't think of them as separate from or operating outside of your relationship with your children. These settings, rules, and limits go hand-in-hand with the focus on relationships you need to build in your home. Ultimately, these technical solutions are simply the more tangible part of the relational solutions.

The right questions to ask when adding technology

We add technology to our homes often. We do it by adding new hardware, new software, or new users.

New hardware

The most obvious way is when we add new hardware — when we buy a completely new device that we have never had before. Examples of this may be an iPad, a Kindle™, an additional phone (for a new user like a teenager), an Apple TV™, a Chromecast™, or some other web-connected device that is new to you or your family.

We also add new hardware when we buy or replace a familiar piece of hardware with a new version that has new features. An example of this would be buying a new television that connects directly to your home's Wi-Fi and has a built in web browser, or a new car that provides its own Wi-Fi hotspot.

New software

We also add technology when we start using a new app or service that we have never used before, such as Facebook, Instagram, TikTok, Hulu, Netflix, or any of thousands of games.

New users

The last way we add technology is when we add users to devices or services that are already in our home. An example of this is when you decide that your 8-year-old can use your phone for games. This can also mean when you decide to allow your children to join a social media site like Facebook or Instagram, or you allow them to post YouTube videos of their video game adventures.

Whether we are adding technology by adding devices, software, or users, we should be asking some important questions about that technology. Unfortunately, most adults ask completely different questions about new technology than children do.

Parent's questions

When adults expand technology, we think about it from an adult viewpoint, and we ask adult-type questions. We are concerned with the benefits of the technology and the reasons behind using it. We also care a lot about the technical details of the product.

We have a list of tasks in our heads that we want the device to do for us. We ask whether the device can do those tasks or whether an updated device can do them better than ever before. The most basic adult technology question boils down to, "What will this device do for me?"

Children don't care about that kind of stuff. They aren't seeking tasks, they are seeking freedom. They don't need the device to do anything specific. They are just in awe of what it might do. Children ask a different question. They ask, "What can it do?"

"What will this do *FOR* me?" vs. "What *CAN* it do?"

These questions might seem similar. But they are very different.

"What will this do *FOR* me?" is pragmatic. It has a purpose and an agenda. It is concerned with tasks. It has a list of qualifications in mind. This question leads to a comparison with the specs of past products. It leads to thinking about measurable outcomes. It involves estimating the cost versus the benefit. It leads to reading the operating instructions carefully.

"What *CAN* it do?" is creative. This question has no agenda or task list. It doesn't care about the intended purpose. This question leads to finding the limits and pushing the edges but it rarely leads to reading the operating instructions. This question leads to unexpected and surprising uses. The only goal of this question is freedom and exploration.

Because our questions are different, they will drive us to use technology in different ways. Let us give you a couple of examples.

What blocks can do

When we give young children blocks, they play with them. They stack them, they arrange them by colors, they build towers, they do a lot of things with them.

Adults look at a child building a tower of blocks and try to read things into it.

"Oh, she's so smart."

"She's so creative!"

"She's going to be an architect."

In fact, that's probably part of why we bought the child blocks in the first place — we are thinking about the blocks from a viewpoint of purpose and goals. We are asking, "What will they do for my child?"

The child just wanted to knock over the tower. The child doesn't even think or care that it looks like a building. She's just testing and exploring. Soon she will be throwing the blocks across the room or feeding them to the dog or trying to flush them down the toilet. Those are definitely "off-label" uses, and if you weren't prepared for them, they can lead to some household drama or even damage. Why do children do things like that? Simple. They are asking, "What can it do?" not "What will it do for me?"

Children are explorers

When you bring technology into your home, children will view it in the same way as they view the blocks. "What can it do?" They will test it, try it, and discover "off-label" uses for it.

Children are natural born explorers. They might have some specific tasks they want to do, but they won't ever stop being explorers. You shouldn't want your children to stop being curious or pushing the boundaries. But that does mean you need to be prepared to be an explorer and think like a child again.

Calculators and becoming explorers again

One piece of good news is that you used to think like a child. And, we have proof.

Before fancy-graphing calculators that children use today, we had plain old ordinary, calculators. Our parents bought them for us after asking a "What can it do *for* me" kind of question. They bought them for a purpose — to help us with schoolwork.

But, we also asked the "What can it do" type of questions. And that is why we all know that we can type into an old calculator 07734, and then hold the calculator upside down to a friend to say, "hello." The old digital screens wouldn't show all the letters of the alphabet, but we worked around it. After learning to say, "hello," we discovered many more things we could say — some appropriate, others... not so much.

Question: Who would think to turn a calculator screen upside down and see if it could spell words?

Answer: Children asking, "What can it do?"

Question: Who would use something intended to do one thing only — math calculations — to communicate with friends?

Answer: Children asking, "What can it do?"

Question: Who would think to create an ersatz language with only eight letters that came to be known as "BEGHILOS"?[13]

Answer: Children asking, "What can it do?"

---

13   "Words you can write on a calculator - The Guardian." 2014. 2 Feb. 2016 <http://www.theguardian.com/education/datablog/2014/jan/10/words-you-can-write-on-a-calculator>

You used to be one of those children.

As we bring new technology into our homes, we need to ask not just the adult questions but the child questions. We need to open up our minds and become explorers again. We need to be prepared and watch out for "off-label" and unadvertised uses for technology. The most important question to ask when adding new technology to your family's life is, "What can it do?"

Once we understand the capabilities of the technology we are bringing into our homes, we need to give purpose to it by shaping our family's interactions with it. In the next chapter we start with you — the parent. There are some specific steps that you as a parent must take to begin shaping and guiding your children's interactions with technology. It starts with conversations and modeling.

CHAPTER 7

WRONG QUESTIONS TO ASK

When I (Titania) allowed my son to start playing on a PS4, I knew I had unleashed Pandora's box. I could literally (OK, figuratively) see the neurons in Jackson's brain rewiring, taking him to a point of no return.

As I struggled with letting him play games and, honestly, the free time it gave me to work and know he was occupied somewhat constructively, I wrestled with a good deal of mom guilt. I knew he was entertained. I knew he was happy in the moment. I also knew that he was sedentary and too much of even a "good" thing could lead to addiction and other health problems.

Whenever I decided he'd played long enough, I would go into the room where he was completely engaged and announce, "OK, that's it. It's time to turn it off. It's time to decompress. It's time to do something productive." Of course, he would either barely acknowledge my presence, or say, "Not right now." Or, if he was in a good mood, he would ask to play for just a few more minutes. He knew that I would tell him to exit his game at least two or three more times before I raised my voice and threatened to smash it with a hammer (or donate it), so he *really* had like 20 more minutes of game time after my first request. When I would ask him, "How much longer do you need to get to a good stopping point?" and, "Why can't you just pause the game?" I was met with grunts and eye rolls and explanations that just didn't make sense. This scenario often ended with yelling, door slamming, and ultimately the loss of all screens anywhere for one full day to — in some cases — up to one month at a time.

Think about how you communicate. You've been communicating your entire life, and for the most part, it has probably worked for you. But in the microcosm of family, confusing communications, missed signals, wrong words, heated emotions, and even careless tones are magnified when mirrored against your children.

Finally, I decided to reframe the problem and the way I addressed it. I remember thinking, *Ah, wrong question, wrong approach, wrong timing.* What does Jackson crave? Control.

In the coming days and weeks, I paid attention to when and what I communicated to my son, and identified the core issue that kept appearing in this situation. I explained to him that when he's playing video games, that gaming console and app store is in control — not him. I explained that much like candy, screens can be addictive, and I want him to always remain in control of his brain. I also explained that sitting for long periods of time can actually kill you! He was ready to listen like never before. This conversation, repeated a few times, gave us both time to shift our perspectives from "Mommy is trying to exert control" to having more meaningful, compassionate, "let's work together" conversations. I ultimately figured out the right questions to ask at the right time.

This same idea holds true with your kids — especially your tweens and teens. The wrong question at the wrong time can shut them down, possibly for days. As your kids grow from helpless babies to unpredictable toddlers to tiny humans who make you laugh and think, you also grow to know your kids' unique personalities, mannerisms, and preferences. Pay attention to them closer than you ever have before.

As they grow through their tweens and teens, our kids change a lot. If we're not paying attention, we may find ourselves more at odds with them than usual because their desire to talk about certain things has lessened. There are certain times of day when they feel more open to hearing from their parents. Sometimes, the day-to-day, or even hour-to-hour, hormone and mood swings are going to make you feel like you're walking across a minefield — one misstep could lead to a blow-up or a shutdown. This is the time that you become the CIA operative for your house and your children. You'll need to keep gathering intelligence on your child every day or week. A lot is happening in their world and within their bodies.

Timing, tone, and the way questions are worded makes a difference in how well your child will open up to you. Now, believe us, you're not going to get this right every day, and we're not asking you to try. You may not be present in a lot of moments. But in the big moments, the situations that need to be addressed, or the problems your child needs to be guided through, those are the times when focusing in and being present during communication is the most important.

As you pay attention to the types of questions you're asking and the ways you're asking them, be mindful of terminology that may cause your kid to shut down. For example, take the term, "parental controls," as an example. This is what most platforms call the settings that parents use to limit their child's access and privileges.

Think about this: In your workplace, what would be the response among employees to an employee handbook if it were titled *Management Controls?* You probably wouldn't want to work for that company. How do you think kids feel — kids who are developing their own self-control and learning what it means to control other things — when you talk to them about parental controls on their devices? More often than not, we're willing to guess that a conversation about control leads to an argument or disagreement between parents and kids. So how do we move from a directive — you can or can't do this — to influence, and allow more freedom as they get older?

We believe in the idea of parental intelligence, not control. What we mean by parental intelligence is the idea that learning the platform — along with learning your child's motivations and behaviors — can be used to inform the expectations and boundaries you set for your child on their devices. Parental intelligence leads to a back-and-forth, open conversation between parent and child. In contrast, a conversation about parental controls leads to struggling, wrestling, and fighting. Not only does this wear away at the familial bonds, but it's exhausting for everyone.

There's a lot of mindfulness and intention that goes into communication with a tween or teen — that is, if you'd like to have an effective conversation. Timing, tone, and terminology are the three Ts that can help guide your conversation to be as productive, open, and honest as possible.

CHAPTER 8

CONVERSATIONS & MODELING

No app, no device, no anything, can influence your child more than you can. That's good for you! When you remove the number of hours your child is in school or at church, and take away the number of hours they play sports or work on hobbies and the number of hours they sleep, it turns out that you have more hours with your kids each year than anyone else. You, the parent, are the primary influence on your child's life.

So, how do you influence your children at home? Two main ways: conversation and modeling.

Conversations lead to discovery

Are you talking to your children regularly? You should be. One of the main ways you influence your children, find out about their world, and discover problems and challenges they face is through conversation.

As parents, we all hear technology horror stories. We hear about children pursued by an online stalker. We hear about children emotionally scarred by and addicted to games or inappropriate content. We hear about children getting bullied online or becoming bullies themselves. When we (Matt and Titania) hear these stories directly from parents, we always ask, "How did you find out about it?" The answer is usually some random occurrence or odd slip-up that tipped off the parent. We then always reply back with one question: "How often do you talk to your children about this very issue?" Having daily conversations with your children — about them, about life, about what is going on in their world — is vital.

Maybe the reason some parents don't know what is going on with their children and technology is that they don't know what is going on with their children at all. Think about all the things your parents didn't know about you — and then magnify that by 100 (given the access kids have today).

Discover the good

Conversation isn't just how you discover bad things in your children's lives, it is the best way to discover the good things in their lives. Through regular conversation, you will get to know your children. You will learn how they react, how they worry, how they think, how they tell stories, and what kind of relationships are in their lives.

Keys to good conversations

Regularity

The first key to having good conversations with your children is regularity, not rarity. This doesn't mean that conversations must happen at the same time of day or the same place every time or even last for more than a few minutes. It does mean that they should be frequent and free-flowing. These simple interactions will have a much bigger impact than scheduled lectures. Regular conversation is exactly the opposite of "sitting your child down for a talk." We all remember getting "talking-tos" and lectures from parents.

They were forced on us. They were one-way communication. They felt accusatory. We were uncomfortable. We just wanted them to be over. In contrast, when you fit regular conversations into the flow of life, they feel comfortable, familiar, and it feels normal to share.

The stuff of life

The second key to conversations with your children is to talk about things that are normal in their world. Talk about the stuff of life — the stuff of *their* lives. When you talk to your children, it's easy to dominate the conversation by telling them what you think they need to know or telling them what to do. It's also easy to ask them leading questions designed to set up the "life lesson" you want to share with them. Instead, your conversations with them need to be focused on them. Don't talk about whether they completed a task, or a school assignment, or what time an extracurricular activity is — talk about them. Talk about their life, not their activities. Talk about their friends, not just their classes. Talk about what is happening in their world. Be curious and show interest in them, and you will be surprised at how much they open up to you.

Questions, but not interrogation

The third key to conversations with your children is asking questions. We talked about this in previous chapters. It's important to ask questions that require something more than regurgitation of information or yes/no answers. You want to ask open-ended questions that aren't directly aimed at getting a single piece of information out of them. "How was your day at school" is going to get a one-word answer: "OK." Instead, try something like "What did you talk about with your friends at lunch today?" to open up a conversation.

Conversation > interrogation

If you talk to your children regularly, you won't have to interrogate them about technology or anything else. Things will just come up normally in conversation. If you talk to your children regularly, you won't have to gain their trust for them to share important things with you. You will already have it. Because of your investment of time talking with them about all the things they think are important, it will only be natural for them to bring important questions to you. If you can make conversations a priority in your home, discovering problems or issues with technology will be just a normal part of discovering problems or issues with anything else in your children's lives.

Modeling it

In order to put conversations first in our homes, we will need to start with ourselves because the other way that we influence our children is through modeling. They will do what they see us doing more often than they'll follow our verbal instructions.

How many times have you come home, sat on the couch, and pulled out your phone or device to stare at it instead of engaging in conversation with your family? Then, every once in a while you show your device to your spouse and say, "Did you see this on Facebook?" Or "Have you seen this meme?"

Great conversation, right?

We know, we know. We're guilty of doing it, too. But no judgment — we're right there with you.

Go thoughtfully through these questions and take a look at your own technology usage before you start trying to think about your children's use of technology.

- Do you view and interact with multiple devices or screens at once? How many at one time, and how often does that happen?
- Have you been watching sports on TV while looking at your fantasy league on a tablet or laptop, and tweeting about the game, while texting

your fantasy league buddies on your phone?

- How often, while driving, do you look at texts, email, or social media at stoplights? (Because you would never look while you are driving, right?)
- How often have you been talking to a person face-to-face, and then stopped talking to them and gave your attention to a notification from your phone? How often has that happened when the person you were talking to was your child?
- How many times in a day is your phone *not* within arms reach?
- When was the last time you sat down for a conversation with a family member and neither of you had a phone or device?
- How many times have you made your children wait while you interacted with a screen instead of them?

Why do we expect our children to behave differently around technology than we do? We expect them to put it down, turn it off, pay attention... but we aren't modeling it. We aren't showing them how. Are we really surprised that children who end up walking like us, shrugging their shoulders the same way we do, or liking the same sports team that we like would get addicted to technology the same way we do?

How to start? A conversation

How can you start modeling a healthy relationship with others and with technology? Start with a conversation with your spouse or a trusted friend. You need to have a conversation about goals. Decide what the goals should be for how often your family sets down the devices, turns off the screens, and makes time for conversation.

The dashboard on a car has a lot of important information about what is happening on your drive. The speedometer tells you how fast you are travelling. The gas gauge tells you how much farther you can go. The temperature gauge tells you if the engine temperature is getting into dangerous ranges.

You need to design a dashboard with gauges for technology use in your home. The first gauges you need to design need to be for you and your spouse. The next ones for your whole family, and the last ones for your specific children. What will be on that dashboard, and what you want the needles to read is up to you, but you need to have a conversation and make a decision to start somewhere.

The good week gauge: What makes a good week?

Here's what my (Matt) wife and I decided. A good week or a bad week depends on one gauge: how many nights a week I am home, around the dinner table with the children, with all the devices off. If our family achieves that four out of seven nights, it's a good week. Anything less than that, it's a bad week. That's one of our gauges of what a good week is for our family, and maybe it would be a good starting place for your family.

Pick a time, turn off the tech, and talk

Your home might need a different gauge or multiple gauges. You might want more nights per week or fewer. Instead of dinnertime you might want a gauge involving breakfast, or an evening walk, or afternoon tea, or drive time. That's fine! Decide what's best for your family, but you have to have the conversation and set the goal. **If you don't have a goal, you'll just drift. And drifting hardly ever leads you to a place you want to be.**

Before my family had a conversation about this, I wasn't home very many times a week for dinner. It wasn't good. It needed to change, but it didn't change until we had a goal set down. Now, we are seeing success. Get specific about when, how long, and how many family conversation times you want to have a week. Set the goal, turn off the tech, and start talking.

CHAPTER 9

CREATION VS. CONSUMPTION

You may remember the story of my (Matt) son in the introduction — how Patriot's behavior began to change as he was exposed more and more to unseemly online content in his peer group. We walked through that difficult season by opening up communication and setting boundaries around screen time. As we navigated how to handle this newly realized technological threat to our family, something interesting occurred — we became curious about the difference between consuming technology and creating technology... or creating anything for that matter.

It's easy and convenient to passively consume. Whether it's TV or music or movies, video games or social media. Consuming those things takes minimal effort. In fact, many people actually use media to numb-out, or disconnect, from the world and from their own reality. Other than giving credibility to someone else's ability to create — in the form of likes or saves or views or hours watched — consuming content is passive and doesn't contribute to the creation of anything.

That is, it doesn't contribute to the creation of anything with the exception of one thing: psychological disruption in the form of anxiety, low self-esteem, fear of missing out (FOMO), and distraction. The only way that consuming content can become active is if it is put to use. Consuming content becomes active when we take what we learn from the content and apply it in a real-world context.

Now, there is some online content that is more instructive and more easily able to be applied in the world than other online content. But even watching a video of someone covering a popular song could teach you how to hold a guitar, or how to hold a microphone, or what sort of capo to use, or how to create vibrato with your voice.

When families become curious about what they're consuming, about what excites them, about what captivates them, they begin to think of ways to create and contribute to the world.

Creating is active, it's living, it's often organic, and it's interpretive. Creating can mean something, or solve a problem, or inspire change. When creating, we're focused, in the flow, rapt, inventive, thinking, busy, making decisions, growing, changing, and learning. When we're creating, we're involved in bringing something to "life," something that consuming will never be able to do.

When our (Matt) family began to focus on creating, we discovered new passions and new talents. As a dad, it was amazing to see Patriot's surprising talents come to the surface — talents we never would've discovered had we not started being curious. One talent in particular was also a dormant (at the time) passion: Christian rap music.

For years, Patriot had listened to Christian rapper, Lecrae. And what he learned from consuming Lecrae's media was rhythm and rhyming, lyric phrasing and dynamics. Up until now, consuming Lecrae's music was all he did with it. When he became curious about it, he started to realize he had a knack for it and began loving it. Soon, his distraction with consuming online content dissipated as he became more and more interested in how to create music.

We began exploring every avenue and relationship we had access to in the music industry. We visited studios, sat in on recording sessions, and even took a turn or two at the microphone. We asked questions, we built a home recording booth, and Patriot began envisioning himself as a creator. As Patriot developed relationships with local studios and artists, he soon made a connection with Lecrae himself.

Before long, Patriot used his savings to purchase equipment and set up a recording space where he wrote lyrics and knit together melodies, harmonies, and beats. Through our connections — now our friends— in the local music scene, Patriot was able to join some up-and-coming rappers on stage during their concert. Then slowly, Patriot started leading at youth events, and eventually he held his own concert.

Now, Patriot has one album already released and is working on his second. He became curious about the right things, his talents and passions emerged, and he has written a better story for himself than one of watching X number of hours on YouTube or creating an unbreakable streak of however-many snaps on Snapchat. Patriot is living outside the screen, and he's contributing at his school and youth groups.

Maybe for some, allowing a child to be curious is a scary proposition, because to be effective, we can't prescribe curiosity. It's not about wanting your child to play piano, so you only let them explore piano. Allowing your child to be curious is about their exploration and discovery of their own talents and passions — with guidance from you. Maybe your child is musical, and has somewhat of an aptitude for playing piano, but they really would rather learn the drums. Help them follow the right kind of musicians on Instagram, or help them engage in appropriate conversations around the hashtags musicians use. With your investment and guidance, you can help your child use social media and technology in the right ways — ways that bring light, encouragement, and inspiration to others.

Everyone can create

With the birth of social media came the easy accessibility for anyone to be able to create. We didn't need to know how to code to create a post or a page on the internet. We didn't need to work for a newspaper to be able to distribute our opinions. We didn't need to break into the radio industry and jockey the 11 p.m. to 7 a.m. dead man's shift. With social media, we opened accounts and started writing, sharing our photographs, sharing our videos, and tagging our friends. People read what we had to say in newsfeeds and timelines — they were consuming the content we were posting. We became content creators.

The tipping point

Around 2011, many social media platforms started to play around with algorithms, which, in essence, has the ability to reorganize a person's social media friends' feed according to most relevant-to-you posts. These preference-based feeds shifted the focus from "most recent," to "assumed relevance" for each user.

Algorithms were controversial at first because many people using social media thought the platforms were dictating what each user was seeing. No longer were users seeing all posts from all friends in chronological order. Instead, they were seeing the most popular and relevant posts from their friends.

As the complexity and dynamic of algorithms evolved over the years, social media feeds became better and better at predicting which posts from your friends you'd want to see more than others. Based on users' likes, link clicks, scroll speed, stops and reverses in the feed, comments, and other factors, the algorithm learned more and more about what images and content were most attractive to us.

The algorithm continues to serve the content it thinks we want to consume, based on the behavior we have exhibited while in the app. With the evolution of the algorithm, consumption began to outpace creation.

Outpacing became imbalance

When the tide of the algorithm came in, the sands of our platform usage shifted. No longer did we add to the conversation, plus keep up with our friends. Instead, we started seeing the popular things, the best things, the prettiest things... or at least the algorithm's best guess at those things for us.

Buried down deeper in our feeds were more of the real things, the untouched photos, the fragmented sentences in a post from a hurting friend. Those things weren't popular. Maybe because they were uncomfortable, or they hit too close to our reality that we didn't want to "Like" them or click the link to read more.

We grew comfortable consuming the pretty, and we began to think things like:

"That is such a cute bathing suit; she looks great. I would look terrible in that."

"Aw, he took his family to Disney World. Weren't they just there last year? I wish I had a life that I could just take off to Disney."

"They look so happy together in their wedding pictures. What a happy life they have. I wish I were happy and getting married."

You get the idea, here. The more we consume, the more our mind takes in these pictures, videos, and lovely written captions as the norm, as if everyone is doing this except for you, you slovenly home body. And that's what our minds will do, they will bring to the forefront the differences between your life and theirs, and your thoughts will tear you down by calling you names and insulting you. An imbalance of consumption will take its toll. It's already linked to anxiety and low self-esteem, as a quick Google search can reveal.

What you and your child can control

The beautiful content we enjoy and the inspirational captions we love to read are being produced by people who are more busy creating than they are consuming. We can't control how much content or what type of content they create. What we can control (and what our children can control) is how much time we spend consuming, how much time we spend creating, what types of content we consume, and our perspectives on all of it.

Defining time spent consuming, time spent creating, and types of content consumed are fairly easy things to determine. They are actual numbers and subjects that are mappable and achievable. However, gaining an appropriate perspective on the posts we see on social media is a more challenging beast to tame. Gaining and then maintaining an appropriate perspective about friends who are "more" than us, "better" than us, "different" than us, even "less" than us sometimes requires focus and constant redirection of our thoughts. **Teaching your child about perspective is one of the most valuable life tools they can develop.**

One of the definitions for perspective in the Merriam-Webster Dictionary is, "The capacity to view things in their true relations or relative importance."

What we don't know is what is going on outside of the frame of that picture, or between the lines of that typed-up story. Because we are human, and because a human created the social media post we are envying, we can take a step back and realize that they have feelings and struggles too. They likely compare themselves to others in some ways. Or maybe they've struggled with their weight, or their finances, or even their marriage.

There are popular memes circulating on social media that feature this quote: "Be kind, for everyone you meet is fighting a hard battle." It's true, we should be kind to others. We don't know what they're going through. But we should also be kind to ourselves. Let's teach our kids to be kind to themselves when they begin to focus on the differences between their real life and the online life of their friends. It's possible for us and for our kids to control thoughts; teach them how to think well of themselves and others.

CHAPTER 10

MOVING FROM CONTROL TO INFLUENCE

We are very familiar with living in a world with limits. We have limits all around us. But for now, let's just look at examples of limits in one area — motor vehicles. We have speed limits and limits on the levels of drugs or alcohol that may be in your system when driving. We have seatbelt laws for cars and trucks and helmet laws for motorcycles. We have requirements on the minimum safety features a car must have, on how long children must ride in a car seat, and on how old a person must be to have a driver's permit and a license.

Some limits are debatable. People have been arguing for years about whether higher speed limits have a negative effect on safety. But some limits are there for a very specific and obvious reason — to prevent us from doing something thoughtless, like not wearing a seatbelt or a helmet, or driving under the influence of drugs and alcohol.

We understand all of these limits in the real, physical world, but somehow when it comes to our children and technology, we don't think

about digital safety in the same way as physical safety. We just turn over the keys and say, "Have fun." That's not the smartest idea. You need to set limits for your family's use of technology.

We all chafe against limits at some point. Undoubtedly, as we begin to talk about the kinds of limits we suggest using with your family, you might find yourself disagreeing. You may even question some of the limits being proposed. That's okay. Don't throw the book across the room quite yet. Just hear us out and try to tell the difference between the limits that might be debatable and the ones that are intended to keep you from doing something thoughtless.

Also, remember to look for the purpose behind the limit. If you can make an adjustment to the limit while still accomplishing the purpose for your family, that would be preferable. But, you need to be open to change and making difficult sacrifices for the long-term benefit of your family. You need to discuss limits with your spouse/co-parent (if applicable) and find a system that you both can agree to enforce. (Note: We're not saying a system your children will necessarily be excited about.)

You wouldn't let your children drive a powerful vehicle out on the open road that is capable of killing them or others without giving them some training and guidance. Wrecking a car isn't the only way your children can wreck their lives. The powerful technology that your children have access to in your home is just as capable of wrecking lives as your car is. So, when they protest, remember that the purpose of these limits is guidance, training, and growth. A plan for growth requires an end goal. Remember the goals you created in chapter one?

The end goal you created in chapter one for each of your children — the purpose for all of these limits and restrictions — is a picture of who your child is by the time they leave your home. When that day comes, they will have *earned* their way to having *no restrictions* on their phone and internet use. The reality is, they aren't ready for that amount of freedom now. They need you to help them get ready, and these limits are part of how you do that.

You're the captain

Staying with the theme of transportation, think about a helicopter and a helicopter pilot. This type of transportation is designed to be amazingly agile and is extremely useful in specific situations. However, generally, a helicopter makes a lot of noise and blows things around when hovering, which causes a mess. It can even get a little unwieldy when maneuvering.

A captain of a ship, on the other hand, has a different set of responsibilities. He or she is responsible for the crew, the passengers, the well-being of the ship. He charts the course and watches the weather conditions. He is at the helm, keeping records, providing direction, and keeping everyone safe on their journey. The captain is also responsible for all the cargo, the loading and unloading, and the embarkation and debarkation of all passengers.

Though both the helicopter pilot and the ship's captain both have very important jobs and responsibilities, you can probably tell from these two descriptions that captaining a ship on a journey is a longer-term role, with more complex moving parts.

You and your spouse or co-parent are the co-captains of your family. You are on a long, sometimes methodical journey to raising adults. There are many moving parts with lots of complexities and dynamics. There is no greater responsibility than guiding a family well through the challenges we face in the 21st century.

You can't do it alone

Though we applaud some parents for having the enthusiasm to monitor their household's technology and social media use on their own, sometimes with spreadsheets and trigger alerts, we know this important work can't be done alone. That's where Bark comes in.

If you don't know Bark yet, let us explain: Bark helps keep more than 5.2 million children across the U.S. safe online and in real life.

Founded in 2015 by CEO (and dad of two) Brian Bason, Bark's award-winning service monitors 30+ of the most popular apps and social media platforms for signs of issues like cyberbullying, suicidal ideation, online predators, threats of violence, and more. It's web filtering and screen time management tools empower families to set healthy limits around the websites and apps their kids can access and when they can visit them.

With Bark Home, parents can bring Bark's powerful screen time capabilities to all of the internet-connected devices in their house — from gaming consoles to smart TVs — providing an unparalleled level of online protection for their family.

After the tragic shooting in Parkland, Florida, Bark decided to extend its services to all K-12 public and private schools in the U.S. — at no cost to them or their communities. Offering content monitoring, web filtering, and a Parent Portal for after-hours alerts, Bark for Schools is trusted by more than 2,400 districts to help protect students from digital dangers.

For a small monthly fee, Bark covers the entire family (unlimited connected accounts and devices), and you can cancel anytime. To give Bark a try, sign up for a seven-day free trial at www.bark.us. (Note: That's not a .com!) Also, as a thank you for reading this book, we'd like to give you a special discount. Use code "PITWBK20" or visit www.bark.us?ref=PITWBK20 to receive *20% off Bark for life.*

Prepare for the excuses

Now, as the captain of your family ship, as you begin to outline boundaries and limits, you're going to run into excuses from your kids.

Your kids probably are accustomed to the rules and limits currently in your home. If so, they probably aren't going to like the changes we're about to suggest. They don't have to.

Here is the main excuse that you are going to get when you try to limit when and where your children can use devices: "But I need my phone in my room all night! I use it for an alarm clock!"

This excuse is classic and follows the format of most excuses your children will try regarding technology: "I need access to this *harmless, mundane, and ordinary function,* so therefore you must give me *free and uncontrolled access to all the functions of this device* so that I may use this harmless, ordinary, mundane function."

This logic is ridiculous. The devices we own do everything, including mundane tasks like functioning as an alarm clock or a calculator or a calendar. But that doesn't mean your children need them to do those tasks. It's simple. Buy a dollar store alarm clock to wake up your child in the morning. He doesn't need 24-hour, unlimited access to a powerful mini-computer in order to wake up on time.

We don't know what creative arguments your children will use as excuses, but don't give in. You might even come up with a few excuses of your own for suggestions of limits that you don't like. When you or your children object to some of these suggestions, look at the objections carefully and analyze them. If your main argument is on behalf of convenience over safety, you probably are looking at an excuse. Most excuses follow a pattern — they suggest abandoning security and wisdom for a little bit of convenience. Don't derail your plans to keep your children and home safe and secure for minor inconveniences and excuses.

Most of the excuses your children will give as objections to limits aren't anything new. They are the exact same excuses you gave your parents for things in the past.

"But all my friends are..."

"Everyone gets to..."

"Other parents don't..."

If you ask around, you will probably find out that none (or most) of that is true. All their friends aren't. Everyone isn't. And the other parents? Most likely, they are struggling just as much as you are. Talk to other parents. You'll probably find out they have the same concerns you do. If possible, work together with other parents to set similar limits and monitor behavior, but don't be pressured by them to cave on the standards you want to set for your family. Remember, you haven't escaped peer pressure just because you aren't in high school anymore. And there is nothing wrong with being the "uncool" mom or "uncool" dad. Bottom line: Be a parent, not a friend. Your children might not like you in the short-term but they will appreciate you in the long-term (when they're older, that is).

Customize your limits

As we talk through the limits, we'll share those that we set for our children in our homes. Your home will be different, so don't feel tied down to our rules. But we hope they will be useful to you as a starting point.

Borders

The first limit involves borders. Borders separate areas from each other. We are familiar with borders between countries, states, and even cities in metro areas. We are also familiar with borders for certain activities. At the park, you can ride your bike on the bike trails, but not on the baseball diamond. Your dog can only be unleashed within the fence of the dog park area. You can smoke in the park, but only in designated smoking areas.

Your home needs borders to designate safe areas for technology to be used by you and by children. As a general rule, this means that no technology will be allowed in a private space. That means no technology should be allowed in bedrooms or any room with a closed door.

In some homes, the children's bedrooms are upstairs, so the border could be the stairs. No technology goes upstairs for any reason. The phones and devices all must be used in the open, downstairs. They all have a place downstairs out in the open where they go at night to charge.

Screen time limits

The use of screens (phones, game systems, televisions, tablets, computers, anything with a screen) needs to be limited by time somehow. There are different ways to do this. You can have a specific time window each day during which technology is not to be used or, reversing that, a time window that is the *only* time technology can be used. You can also have a certain amount of time that the children are freely able to use as they wish. This is a little harder to enforce without some technological help to track the usage, but it is a great system that gives them a little more freedom.

In my (Matt) home, my children have thirty minutes when they first get home to use technology for homework. Their school uses an online system for them to retrieve and complete assignments on a computer or tablet. Then, for the rest of the evening, they have 90 minutes of screen time that they can use whenever they want. During that time, they also have to eat dinner (no screens during that time), do chores, spend some time outdoors, and sometimes other activities. Both individual and family activities count against their time. So if we watch sports, a TV show, or a movie as a family, that counts as part of their screen time.

In my (Titania) home, we are a bit more loosey-goosey. My husband and I have one child, and thanks to virtual learning, he's in front of a screen out of necessity for longer than we'd like. Our goal, based on conversations with child health specialists, is to make sure Jackson does not spend more than two hours at a time in front of a screen without a break. We encourage outside play as much as possible, discourage the use of screens during dinner (in the rare times we actually all sit down together at the same time), and turn off tech at (ideally) 30 minutes before it's time for bed. We don't allow internet-connected devices in his bedroom and utilize Bark's screen time feature to shut everything down at 11 p.m. (internet AND LTE!), just in case my husband and I fall asleep before our night owl.

You need limits too

As you impose limits on your children, remember that you need to be modeling how to deal with limits. To do that, your kids need to see the limits you set affecting what you do. Your limits don't have to be the same as theirs, but they need to be observable by your children in their normal lives. For example, at least part of your "no phone" time needs to happen before your children go to bed, so they can see you put the phone down and choose to spend time with them. You might need to wear a watch or put clocks around the house so you don't use the excuse of "I need my phone as a timepiece." **Your children need to see you getting text messages in the car while driving, but not looking at them or responding.** This isn't just about their sense of fairness, it's about training them. You need to model it for them or they won't understand how to do it. If you don't model it, it will be very difficult to get them to stick to the limits you set.

The difference between tensions and problems

In our lives, we depend heavily on technology for different things that we do. You may need to stay in touch for work. You may own your own business that requires after-hours work. You may have clients (or bosses) who blow up your phone all night long with after-hours email questions.

When it is your livelihood that causes a need to stay in touch, it makes it very hard to totally shut things down. These types of adult realities can make for some difficult tensions in our lives, and we need to recognize that. Let your children know what is going on when you wrestle with these things. If work emails or phone calls are interfering with technology downtime with your family, make sure when you step away for an email that must be answered that you don't also glance at Facebook, or send a text message. It's okay to let them see you struggling and fighting to keep technology from intruding on your time.

We will all have tensions that we have to manage moment by moment. Some things, however, aren't tensions. They are problems. Tensions can be managed. Problems need to be solved. When the issue is consistent, and when it starts damaging how you are connecting with your family and how you are modeling the use of technology to your children, that is an issue that is becoming more than a tension to manage. It's a problem, and you will need to set some kind of limit to solve it.

Problems like this will often come up in an area of weakness for you. I (Matt) don't know what your weak areas are, but I had a problem with a game.

It started as an attempt to spend more time with my boys. We were playing a cooperative game during their screen time. I thought that it would be cool to play the game with them. I'd be spending time with them. Part of their 90 minutes of screen time would still be "dad time." It was cool for a while, but after their screen time was up, and they went to bed... I wouldn't stop playing the game. I'd keep playing, racking up achievements and points. Then I'd talk to them later and say, "Did you see the cool thing I did in the game?" Their response was grumpy. "We could if you gave us more screen time," they said. They had a right to be grumpy.

I had taken something we were doing together and allowed it to become something that I did without them for my own enjoyment. In the end, this wasn't a tension I could manage. It was a problem. I wasn't modeling for my children what I wanted to model. Because I couldn't do that, I stopped playing the game. In fact, I deleted all games off my phone completely.

You will be different. Your weakness will be different. You will have to come up with your own solution. Our problems with technology addiction often have to do with some weakness that is unique to us.

Maybe you just can't stop checking your email every time it dings because you love being the office hero and being the one to save the day.

Maybe you are escaping into YouTube as a distraction from work frustrations.

Maybe you can't stop looking at Pinterest and imagining your home as you wish it could be.

Whatever your point of difficulty, find it and set yourself a limit. Part of teaching our children about limits is modeling how to live within limits ourselves. Sometimes the most important limits we can set are around the things that we enjoy the most. And yes, that includes Netflix and Instagram (Titania's favorites).

Mistakes will be made

No matter how many limits or boundaries are set, and no matter how many open conversations you have by using the right question at the right time to instill confidence and cause creativity, your kids are going to mess up. They will go beyond the limit you've set. Or they'll find something untoward that you haven't set a limit on yet.

Some of your kids like to know what the rules are, or what is expected, so that they can test how to get around them. At first, they will comply. They may jump through the hoops, or limits, you've set very well at first. Then, they'll start sliding. Maybe they'll go over screen time by 30 minutes. Or maybe they'll send a flirty private message to a boy or girl they like, and maybe they'll send an inappropriate picture. Your kids are going to mess up. They are kids. They are not tiny adults (despite having more access to information than any adult ever did before the internet). The part of their brains that guides reasoning is not fully formed until their early 20s!

Your job is to help them through their mess-ups. Your job is not to fix anything for them or bulldoze their path. Your job is to help them navigate the sometimes rocky path that looms before them. In essence, you are raising adults who will be captains of their own family ships someday. Honor their future by helping them navigate hard things now, while you have this special influence on their lives.

CHAPTER 11

THE TECH SPECTRUM

It's amazing how scientific development follows the path laid out by our fictional dreams of both the distant and near future. Jules Verne's novel, *From the Earth to the Moon*, was published in 1865. In 1902, it inspired the first science fiction film, Georges Méliès' *A Trip To The Moon*. Then, only 104 years after Verne's novel, we made the fantasy real with the Apollo moon landing. NASA even chose a similar launch location as in the fictional Verne story. Kennedy Space Center was built on the eastern coast of Florida while Jules Verne had described the giant gun to fire his protagonists to the moon being built on the western coast of Florida. Science fiction hasn't just inspired new realities in huge, space-exploring government agencies. It inspired the men and women who built the devices and technologies that now fill our homes and pockets.

If you were born in the 1970s, you were born in the decade when pocket calculators first became available. You have never lived in a world in which you couldn't carry a calculator in your pocket. That was a big deal then. In the 1970s, a computer as powerful as the iPhone was the size of a house or barn. Obviously, technology has greatly developed since we were younger, but it isn't just about the amount of technological change. It is the pace of this technological change. Today, technology is changing exponentially faster.

I (Matt) happened to be born in what was then called the "gap" generation. We were after Generation X, but weren't yet Generation Y. We were in transition. I learned to type on a typewriter. Just four years later, I was learning programming in a computer lab and dying of dysentery as I made yet another attempt to complete Oregon Trail. In just four years, a massive shift happened, and the technology I had just learned how to use was already obsolete. Around the same time, when a friend of mine started college, it was really weird (even for an engineering major) that one of his first roommates had a personal computer in the dorm room. But by the time my friend's younger brother came along just five years later, it was nearly unthinkable that any college student could get by without a personal computer. That's some pretty fast technological and cultural change.

Today, the rate at which technology advances is even faster. Every year, we get new devices with powerful new capabilities (or improvements on the abilities they had previously). Whatever new technology your children learn this year will be replaced or outdated next year. Something new and relatively unknown today, in six months, might be dominating the market and the world, and in six more months, completely disappear. This speed of development is called Moore's Law,[14] which says that the number of transistors on a microchip doubles every two years, while the price of computers goes down. Gordon E. Moore made this prediction in 1965, and it proved itself true over the years — with one slight difference. The rate that transistors are being doubled on microchips is closer to 18 months.

Moore's Law has extended beyond transistors and circuits into the fast-paced world of social sharing, something Mark Zuckerburg labeled as

---

14   https://www.investopedia.com/terms/m/mooreslaw.asp

the Law of Sharing.[15] The Law of Sharing says that the average amount of information that a person shares doubles every year or so.

Let's take a look at this concept through the lens of the technology developed in just the past century. As the decades pass, you can witness the number of breakthroughs, new devices, and groundbreaking inventions increase at an incredible clip — right up until the present — and things certainly show no sign of stopping.

1920s
- Modern electronic television invented
- Optical character recognition scanning systems first developed
- Electric refrigerator invented

1930s
- Color television invented
- First solar-powered house
- Xenon flash lamp invented for high-speed photography
- Principle of photocopying is invented

1940s
- Proposal of a desk-sized memory store called Memex; some features later incorporated into electronic books and the World Wide Web
- Communications satellite conceived that can bounce radio waves from one side of Earth to the other
- Invention of the transistor, allowing electronic equipment to be made much smaller
- Barcodes are patented

---

15   https://www.wired.com/2013/04/facebookqa/

1950s

- Fiber optics pioneered
- TV remote control invented
- First integrated circuit developed
- Design Augmented by Computers-1 (DAC-1) — first computer-aided design (CAD) system — developed

1960s

- Light-emitting diode (LED) invented
- Sketchpad developed, one of the first computer-aided design programs
- Airline ticket reservation system, SABRE, developed
- Dynamic random access memory (DRAM) invented
- An electronic book, nicknamed Dynabook, is imagined
- Charge-coupled device (CCD) — the light-sensitive chip used in digital cameras, webcams, and other modern optical equipment — invented
- Astronauts walk on the moon
- First computer mouse developed
- Compact discs invented

1970s

- First single-chip computer (microprocessor) built
- First handheld cell phone developed
- Linking computers together via ethernet is developed
- First purchase of an item using a barcode
- Home automation system developed
- Apple 1 computer launched — one of the world's first personal computers
- Discrete Cosine Transform (DCT) compression technique proposed, going on to become the most widely used data compression algorithm in social media
- Talkomatic chat room application created
- TERM-Talk instant messaging application is created

- PLATO Notes conferencing and bulletin board forum system created
- ARPANET evolved into the internet

1980s

- First truly portable player for recorded music, the Sony Walkman, is developed
- Space Shuttle makes its maiden voyage
- Patent files for flash memory — reusable computer memory that can store information when the power is off
- Compact discs (CDs) are launched as a new way to store music
- DLP Projectors developed
- World Wide Web invented
- Bulletin Board System (BBS) emerges as one of the earliest forms of social media
- FidoNet forms as BBSs start to exchange email in North America and later internationally

1990s

- MEGA 1, the world's first radio-controlled wristwatch, is introduced
- VoIP invented for sending telephone calls over the internet
- Broadcast.com becomes one of the world's first online radio stations
- eBay auction website is launched
- First high-definition television signal in the United States is broadcast
- Wi-Fi becomes a worldwide standard for wireless internet
- Bolt.com was started as the first social networking and video website
- Social networking website SixDegrees.com is created
- AOL Instant Messenger is released
- Open Diary launches the first social blogging network, inventing reader comments and friends-only content
- Yahoo! Messenger launches
- MSN Messenger launches
- LiveJournal — an early blogging platform and social network — launches

2000s

- Apple iPod MP3 music player is released
- Wikipedia is launched
- BitTorrent file sharing is developed
- iRobot releases its first Roomba vacuum cleaning robot
- Amazon.com launches Kindle electronic book (ebook) reader
- Apple introduces touch-screen cell phone called the iPhone
- Habbo, a game-based social networking site, launches
- Social networking and gaming site Friendster launches
- Business-oriented social networking service LinkedIn launches
- Social networking website Hi5 launches
- Business-oriented social networking website XING launches
- Myspace launches
- Skype instant messaging and video/voice calling service launches
- Facebook launches
- Flickr launches
- Orkut, a Google-owned social networking site, launches
- Tagged, a social discovery website, launches
- Bebo, a social networking website, launches
- Reddit, an American social news aggregation, web content rating, and discussion website, launches
- Twitter launches
- Tumblr, a microblogging and social networking website, launches
- FriendFeed, a real-time social media feed aggregator, launches
- Justin.tv, a live-streaming site that allowed anyone to broadcast video online, launches

2010s

- Apple releases touch-screen tablet computer, the iPad
- 3D TV starts to become more widely available
- Elon Musk announces hyperloop, a giant, pneumatic tube transport system

- Supercomputers (the world's fastest computers) are now only 30 times less powerful than the human brain
- Apple Watch introduced
- Miniature machines are built out of molecules
- Google claims to have achieved quantum supremacy with a quantum computer that calculates faster than a conventional one
- Pinterest launches
- Instagram launches
- Path launches
- Quora launches
- Snapchat launches
- Google+ launches
- Keek launches
- Twitch launches
- Tinder launches
- Vine launches
- Google Hangouts launches
- Musical.ly launches
- Periscope launches
- Beme launches
- Meerkat launches
- TikTok launches

That's a lot of technological advancements over the last 100 years. It's interesting to see how technological breakthroughs going back as far as the 1920s laid a foundation for future launches. The ability to compress images and data leading to the development of algorithms was developed 50 years ago. In more recent decades, we can see the increase in developments, inventions, and launches, indicating that the pace of technology is gaining speed. There's no way we will be able to keep up with how often it changes, what features are changing, how many social networks are launching, and how we'll use these advancements to communicate, create, share, and consume.

Now, the realization that we'll never be able to keep up with all the changes to technology as they happen and are launched is not a justification for standing idly by while our children run around unsupervised on these developing networks and communication methods. We have to do our best to set boundaries on the networks we've decided to allow.

The dreams

So much of today's technology is like wish fulfillment of the gadgets we loved from science fiction movies and TV shows we grew up watching. Our heroes took us into their homes, businesses, and secret hide-outs that were full of wonderful, imaginative technology that we wished and hoped would be in our homes soon. And now, many of those dreams have, indeed, become part of our lives and our homes.

Star Trek® communicators became flip phones, and now, our smartphones are practically tricorders. We use them to explore our world as they feed us all kinds of location-based information, and even take readouts from health management devices that monitor our sleep patterns, activity levels, and pulse rates.

Ever since Dick Tracy® did it, we've been wanting to chat with people on our watches. Thanks to Apple Watch® and others, we finally can.

Siri® from Apple®, Cortana® from Microsoft®, and Alexa® from Amazon® might not be quite as slick as the computer from Star Trek or Jarvis® from Iron Man®, nor as loveable as C-3PO® or R2-D2®, but smart, robotically voiced assistants that understand you, answer you, and find you the information you need are here to stay, and they are getting smarter and better every year.

The Jetson's® flat-screen television became, well, flat-screen televisions. And they are getting even thinner every year. The Jetson's robotic vacuum cleaner became the Roomba®. Also, remember when the Jetsons would push a button and the food or product they wanted would show up at their house? Amazon now has "Dash Buttons™" that you can put in the places where you store commonly purchased items such as laundry detergent or mac and cheese. Just push the Dash Button for that specific item, and Amazon will send a refill to your house. In many places, the delivery will even be on the same day.

The nightmares

The dreams of science fiction aren't the only things we have brought to life with technology. Some of the horrible threats to humanity imagined in science fiction have also become real threats that we are currently navigating.

The introduction of reality television, the effects of environmental pollution on the poor, and the method of terrorism used by the 9/11 hijackers were all predicted by Stephen King's 1985 novel *The Running Man.*

No one has yet created a rampaging herd of raptors, but scientists are currently pursuing many of the cloning techniques forecast in Michael Crichton's *Jurassic Park.*

The global problems of inequality and inequity explored in the 1927 film *Metropolis* and in *The Time Machine* by H. G. Wells are part of our current political struggles.

The security of information and free speech are very much under threat today, bringing the fictional worlds from George Orwell's *1984,* and Ray Bradbury's *Fahrenheit 451* frighteningly close to reality.

Why is this important?

Technology isn't just some magical solution to our problems. It also isn't some soulless evil that has come to destroy us. Both the world of dreams and the world of terrors are made possible by technology. That is because technology is just an extension of our nature — a result of our efforts to solve the problems we encounter in life. Technology penetrates our lives and culture, not because it is part of an evil plot, but because it is answering problems that we struggle with every day.

Think about the technology you use each day when you leave your house, the problems those technologies help you solve, and how that technology has changed.

From two pockets to three pockets

Men used to pat two pockets when they left their houses — checking that they had their wallet and keys with them. Now they pat three pockets. You probably do something similar. Why? Because we added a third "thing" that is a vital part of our lives. Our phones, our technology, have now become as vital to us as our wallet and keys. These items each represent an area of our world that we need to have access to in daily life.

Wallet = Economic access — Your wallet gives you access to the economy. Everywhere you go, you carry identification and the means to purchase goods and services.

Keys = Physical access — Whether it is shelter (your home), belongings (storage), or transportation (vehicle), you carry with you the means to access the places you go and your means to get there.

Phone/device = Relationship and information access — Our devices connect us to any person and any piece of information we need, at any time that we need it.

The phone as the third "thing" we carry is not the result of some new-fangled whim but of a desire for connection to knowledge and relationships that humans have always had. We have always wanted communication and information at our fingertips. It's why we created writing, the printing press, books, and libraries. It's why there used to be pay phones on almost every corner. It's why we were once able to call any business, restaurant, hotel, or airport and leave a message for someone or even have them paged to come to a wired "courtesy phone" for calls. It is why we relied on physical messenger services, like couriers, to carry vital, daily business communication. The persistent desire to be connected and to have constant access to people and information is not new. It's just that we now have the technology that makes it possible.

Soon you will be patting two pockets again, then only one pocket

The days of patting three pockets on the way out the door are... on the way out the door. Our devices are in the process of absorbing the capability of economic access. You can go almost anywhere now and pay with your phone using one of many methods. The wallet is going digital.

Physical access isn't that far behind. There are already doors and locks that can be opened by your phone or other device without needing a key. To open our front doors with our phones, all we have to do is pay for and install the new hardware — the new doors or door knobs.

Every "thing" we've always wanted

But it isn't just your daily carry items that are changing. Every "thing" in your home will soon be a part of a network of data-gathering, recording, reporting, interconnected devices. If you haven't heard the term, "The Internet of Things" is a term that refers to the network of connected appliances, gadgets, and devices that are able to exchange data with each other through the internet — think smart TVs, digital thermostats, and smart speakers. More and more common household items, articles of clothing, and appliances are starting to include features that connect to the internet in some way.

All of these items are amazing and have the ability to help us organize and control our lives in ways we couldn't do even just a few years ago. They are, quite literally, the products of our imaginations made real. But these things also bring with them dangers. How do we deal with our simultaneous attraction to, and fear of, technology? How do we separate the dreams from the nightmares?

What should our response be?

There are at least three paths we can take.

The path of acceptance

The path of acceptance is the path the majority of families are on. On this path, we try everything right out of the box. We become early-and-often adopters. We stand in line for the newest tech. We *never* read the End User License Agreements — we just click "Accept." We jump in and go along with all the latest trends, tech, and culture. We don't worry, we just enjoy the ride and hope nothing goes wrong.

The problem with this path is that it puts too much trust in technology, culture, and the government that regulates them to keep us safe. Governments don't move quickly and technology does. Regulation takes years, decades even. Think about how many people died before the government started forcing us to wear seatbelts or put a warning label on cigarettes or regulate leaded gasoline and paint. The path of acceptance is a fun ride, but it can end in tragedy.

The path of rejection

On the path of rejection, we reject dangerous, cutting-edge technology. We withdraw from the new. We have a "dumb" phone (and are, sometimes, puritanically proud of that fact). We do not participate in new devices, communication methods, or the culture that they create and support.

There's an entire culture here in the United States that decided a long time ago to opt out of further technology. They didn't do it out of fear but out of a desire for simplicity. They drew the line at zippers and horseless carriages.

Zippers? That's too much technology. Buttons are the most advanced clothing technology we need.

Horseless carriages? Nope. Horses and buggies can take me anywhere I need to go, thank you very much. If my horse and buggy can't get me there, maybe I don't need to go.

And, do you know what? They are exactly right. You don't *need* zippers. You don't *need* trucks or cars. You don't *need* mobile devices or computers. This is a perfectly valid choice you can make about technology and culture, but you can probably tell we wouldn't make that choice, and we don't think you or your children would either.

Here's why we don't make this choice: We're less worried about ourselves and our children being influenced by the culture than we are about the members of our families not having a voice in the culture around us.

You can drive up to the countryside in Pennsylvania and buy some fantastic furniture or quilts from people who only travel in horse-drawn buggies. We could and should learn a lot from these communities about sustainability and the stewardship of resources. They have a lot to teach us about the benefits of quietness, meditation, humility, and living simply. However, you won't find these communities having a huge effect on culture outside of their immediate surroundings. That is because radically withdrawing from technology means radically withdrawing from culture, and it is difficult to have a voice in a culture from which you have radically withdrawn.

The path of relationship

On the path of relationship, we enter the world of new technology with care, with mindfulness, and with an intentional, relationship-centered purpose. With new technologies we go slowly and test carefully. We allow our relationships to give purpose to our technology usage and never let technology disrupt the purpose of our relationships. On this path, our relationships can benefit from the power of technology instead of being wrecked by it, and through our relationships outside the family, we have a voice in the culture of our friends, schools, communities, and ultimately, the world.

This is the path we hope to help you and your family choose by reading this book.

Technology is not the hero of our dreams or the villain of our nightmares

Technology is not the problem. We are. Technology is amoral — neutral. But technology is also a mirror. The story of technology, both the good and the bad, is a story about us. When we look in the mirror of technology, we don't just see how it changed the world, we see how it changed us. We are different because of the way technology has developed. As it changed, it changed us, too.

Ignorance isn't an option

Modern parenting is hard. There will be some days when you feel confident and encouraged in your efforts to raise a well-rounded adult. Then other days you will fail yourself, and you will fail them. Managing technology and social media in the home is a lot — it's a huge responsibility. Accepting that there will be ups and downs as you navigate boundaries for your children helps to frame your mindset to not beat yourself up — most days.

The alternative to being intentional, setting boundaries, and asking questions is willful ignorance. And that's unacceptable. That's a disservice and a dishonor to your child's development of handling responsibility, managing relationships, and leading their own family one day.

CHAPTER 12

TIRED OF KEEPING UP

Okay. You are going to do this thing. You are going to take control of your family's tech setup and keep them safer online. You look around your house. You start to think about all the ways your kids can connect to the internet. Initially, you think you can list them on your fingers. Actually, you'll soon be overwhelmed, and you'll realize you need to make a list. You get a pen and paper and get to work.

- Television (living room)
- Television (parent's bedroom)
- Television (basement)
- 8-year-old's Nintendo 3DS
- Nintendo Switch
- Wii
- PS4
- Family iPad mini
- Mom's old iPhone in the kitchen drawer
- 11-year-old's Palm
- 11-year-old's Chromebook for school
- 8-year-old's flip phone
- Dad's phone

- Mom's phone
- Ring doorbell
- Amazon Alexa
- The office computer
- Mom's laptop
- Dad's laptop
- Dad's iWatch

You realize this is going to take a while. You wonder if there is a "Geek on Call" for this kind of thing. (There is by the way — we'll tell you about it at the end of this chapter). You start with the TVs as that will knock three items off the list... you think.

First of all, who knows where the owner's manuals are for any of the TVs, but you're at least aware there is a settings menu . . . somewhere. On the newest TV in the living room, the menu is easiest to find — there's a menu button on the remote. You pull up the menu, find settings, then find parental controls. On the parental controls screen, there is a list — a long list — of toggle switches for each available option. One by one, you make your selections. Your final move — for this first TV — is to set up a four-digit code to lock in these controls.

The television in your bedroom is older, and there are buttons on the bottom of the set that bring up different options. You scroll through the options, only to discover that there aren't as many options for limiting children's access to inappropriate content on this television. Note to self: Update television in bedroom.

The television in the basement is a projector aimed at a large screen, and it's one of those movie-theatre setups called Connect-It-All or something like that. The remote control is much more complicated, but after some time of clicking on lights, then dimming lights, then turning off the lights, then turning on the projector, and accidentally turning on the lights again, and then finally bringing up the main menu... well, now you're fully lost, because the menu is listing words and options you know nothing about. You decide to leave this one for your partner or that tech-savvy babysitter and you put an asterisk next to it on your list.

Okay, TVs... sort of complete. Moving on to gaming devices. Hmmm. The PS4 is hooked up to the projector in the basement, so you add another asterisk beside that item on your list because you clearly don't know how to access the projector system in order to access the menu of the PS4.

The Wii on the television in the living room should be simple enough. You turn everything on, and get the opening screen of the Wii when you realize you're going to have to navigate the Wii menu with the game controller — which isn't always as straightforward as your television remote. After bouncing around for a few minutes, you find the parental controls section in Settings, and you're faced with a list of features with toggle buttons. One by one, you make your selections and create a password to lock down your choices.

Well, after an hour and a half, you have three devices set up correctly out of the 20 items on your list. At this pace, it will take you 10 hours to set up all of your devices. You soldier on.

For the Nintendo DS, you decide to disconnect it from the internet altogether. You find the account, you set up a PIN, security question, and your email address, and you remove it from the Wi-Fi. Easy enough. You repeat the process for the Nintendo Switch. At least the two of these devices took only 20 minutes; maybe you can get the rest of this done before the kids get home at 4. Ugh. But there's so much more to do.

Next, you round up the phones. You can mark off the flip phone from your list because it doesn't have Wi-Fi anyway, but you need to review your son's settings on his Palm. You turn it on and look through it, and aside from some mild inappropriate language that he's sending via text, it doesn't appear that anything else is going on. You make a note on your list to talk to him about language. You check the settings and see that they are still the way you left them when you originally set up the phone, but you reset the PIN that accesses the settings, just in case.

Now onto the laptops and iPads. You're at least a little more familiar with these since you work on a laptop all day. On the iPad, you navigate to the General Settings screen, set up a lock code, a security question, and begin to make your choices for the limitations of the family iPad. All items are saved and you move on to you and your partner's laptops. Knowing that both of you will need the ability to download large files, use text messaging apps, and the like, you decided that locking the laptops completely with the use of a security code is the best option. Yours is already set up that way, but you decide to go ahead and change it just in case you had given your password to your kids on a previous occasion. There. All done, laptop number one.

Your partner's laptop already has a passcode, so you add an asterisk to his laptop on your list so that you can remember to ask him to change his code. Your hopes of having all of these items complete in one fell swoop is dashed as you realize your partner will need to complete his items on the list. But you're determined to knock out as much as you can.

It's now 2 p.m. and your partner and the kids will be home from soccer practice around 4 p.m. From your son's backpack, you pull out his Chromebook and review the settings you created when you gave it to him a year ago. Your password to the parental controls could stand to be updated, so you change the password and make a note of the new one.

You consider tackling the Ring doorbell, but you'd rather your partner take that one on since he set it up originally. You add an asterisk next to that item on your list.

For Amazon Alexa, you open your app on your iPhone and access each particular device's settings to control the Amazon FreeTime settings. As with all things Amazon seems to do, it's simple and takes just a few minutes to set up from your iPhone app for all devices in the house.

Before you can reach for the last item or two on your list, you hear your family in the garage, arriving home. Soon, everyone busts through the door with shouts of "Hello," and the clamor for snacks and devices starts. You didn't even stop for lunch as you scurried from room to room.

As you greet everyone and send them off to change clothes, you tell your kids that they have one hour of free time before they need to report to the kitchen for dinner duty. Groans, moans, and general rebellious body language commences.

At 5 p.m., the kids report for dinner duty. And when everyone sits down to dinner — food is on the table, grace has been said, and forks are clinking — you begin to share how you spent your day, and what upated boundaries have been placed on everyone's devices. Your 11-year-old is the most annoyed, saying it's unfair, and that other parents don't do this.

Through many twists and turns, high emotions and tears, your family has a meaningful conversation about boundaries and devices. Not everyone is happy, especially not the kids... and maybe your partner since he plays some games with friends occasionally. But at least everyone is informed and educated.

As everyone cleans up dinner and heads their separate ways for the evening, you hand the list of devices with your notes to your partner, asking him to update the items with an asterisk next to them. As a network engineer in his day job, it takes him about 30 minutes to finish up the list while you begin the process of shopping for a new television for your bedroom.

A lot to manage

We don't pretend that this isn't a lot to manage — more technology than any parents ever had to manage in the history of parenting. First, every home has a lot of devices that connect to the internet — it's the world we live in. Second, not many of us are tech professionals, capable of knowing the full extent of what each and every device is capable of. And third, because most of us aren't tech professionals, we sometimes don't recognize the terminology used in the parental control settings or in the descriptions of the device's features.

But there is a solution out there. Sometimes a company makes things fairly simple to set up, like with the Amazon devices in your home all accessible through one app. But each platform is separate, and settings may be in different locations in the menu.

This is where the **Barkomatic**[16] — an all-in-one parental control resource — comes in.

You already know that Bark is your internet safety solution. It's an essential tool for helping to keep kids safe while they navigate growing up in a tech world. Today's kids face challenges unlike ever before, and digital technologies only complicate the matter.

---

16   https://bark-o-matic.com/

By monitoring texts, email, YouTube, and more than 30 social media platforms, Bark alerts parents to signs of cyberbullying, depression, suicidal ideation, sexual predators, and more.

Keeping your kid safer online — and in real life — is an ongoing project. But monitoring with Bark helps parents protect their kids from digital dangers.

One of Bark's free resources is the Barkomatic — the internet's first customizable resource for parental controls. No matter how your child uses the internet, the Barkomatic can provide you with all the information you need quickly, easily, and in one location. In three steps, you get personalized instructions for every device in your home.

Step one: Tell Barkomatic what your child uses. Simply select all of the different ways your child accesses the internet, and it will do the rest.

Step two: Barkomatic activates. The Barkomatic will analyze your selections and pull information and instructions from across the web.

Step three: Get custom results. When it's done, Barkomatic will email you the link for your results — just click and you can begin setting controls.

Step four: After receiving your custom results, what's next? Once the Barkomatic has generated your personalized results, you will be taken to your results page with step-by-step instructions for each device and social platform. All instructions, all in one place. Remember the hours you spent searching for settings menus and parental controls? Gathering these instructions took less than three seconds for Barkomatic.

Step five: Once your personalized instructions are gathered, you also can explore Bark's useful resources for best practices to help your kids stay safe online and in real life.

The only thing constant in life is change, and as your family acquires new gadgets, downloads new apps, and grows in maturity, you will want to reevaluate your tech policies and settings. Here are some of our favorite, trusted resources to help you stay informed and ultimately keep your kids safer online:

Create a technology contract:
https://www.bark.us/blog/tech-accountability-create-technology-contract-family/

Watch *Childhood 2.0*, a free and incredibly compelling documentary about growing up in the digital age:
https://www.childhood2movie.com/

Follow Protect Young Eyes, an amazing team that helps create safer digital spaces:
https://protectyoungeyes.com/

Read "Kids and Technology: How to Help Keep Them Safe Online":
https://www.bark.us/blog/kids-and-technology-safety/

Review "Email for Kids: How to Create a Safe Account":
https://www.bark.us/blog/email-account-for-kids/

Get familiar with the top five social media apps parents should monitor:
https://www.bark.us/blog/top-5-social-media-apps-parents-monitor/

Learn how to talk about online predators with your kids:

https://www.bark.us/blog/online-predators-talk-kids/ as well as https://www.bark.us/blog/protect-child-online-predators/

Check out "The Ultimate Guide to Gaming and Chatroom Safety":
https://www.bark.us/blog/ultimate-guide-gaming-chatroom-safety/

Go over these basic internet safety tips:
https://www.bark.us/blog/teaching-internet-safety-kids/

If and when your child does get a smartphone, be sure to review this first:
https://www.bark.us/blog/first-phone-tips-tools/

Sign up for a free, one-week trial of Bark to monitor your child's social media, email, and text messages, filter inappropriate content, and manage screen time (receive 20% off for life with code PITWBK20):
https://www.bark.us/

Join Parenting in a Tech World, the closed Facebook group dedicated to discussing all of these issues (and more):
https://www.facebook.com/groups/parentinggeeks/

Follow Bark Technologies on Instagram for quick tips and updates on all things parenting and tech:
https://www.instagram.com/barktechnologies/

There is enough exhausting navigation in parenting without the foreboding task of keeping up with parental controls on apps and devices. Let Bark work its magic through Barkomatic to help you keep your family safer online.

CHAPTER 13

PASSWORDS ARE DOORWAYS

Parents typically have good instincts about how to keep their children safe in the physical world. We keep them in sight. We know when silence means there is a problem. We watch for suspicious people in public places. We hold their hands to keep them close in crowded spaces or dangerous areas.

We also work hard to put as many barriers between our family and the dangers of the world as possible. But somehow when it comes to a child's safety in the digital world, some parents lose their good instincts and don't put up any barriers. All of those things you naturally do to protect your children in the physical world add up to one main thing in the digital world — controlling your child's passwords.

You need to know and control your child's passwords

Passwords are doorways allowing your child access to digital spaces and anyone who may be present in those spaces. If you don't control your child's passwords, there is no way to control where your child goes, what he sees, who sees her, what he buys, or what she experiences. You are leaving the doors and windows unlocked and wide open.

The internet as an intersection; hold their hands

Think about it this way. How would you walk with your children across a busy and dangerous intersection? You would hold their hands. Tightly. It wouldn't matter how much those tiny hands squirmed and wanted to walk alone through the traffic, you wouldn't let go. Why? *Because the potential for disaster and tragedy if your children made a small mistake in judgment is life-altering.*

On the internet, a small error in judgment can be just as devastating as stumbling into traffic. The internet is the biggest, most dangerous, fastest, most ridiculous intersection that has ever existed. Any internet-capable device is a gateway to walking across it. Knowing your children's passwords is walking across a busy intersection while holding their hands. Anything less is pushing them into traffic and saying, "Good luck, honey."

But don't they need privacy?

Not when it comes to passwords. Don't be swayed by those who wish to argue that young children have a right to the privacy of their passwords. Children don't need privacy on that scale. Children need to be alone every once in a while and have some space they feel is theirs, of course — but that's not the same as you not knowing their passwords. You not knowing their passwords means absolute privacy. Do they need that? Absolutely not.

Knowing their passwords has a purpose

Don't forget that you're the parent. You are responsible for controlling the flow of information into their devices and into their minds. You can't do that without controlling the passwords.

When you don't have their passwords, you don't have access to all the information that your child has access to. You need that access so that you can guide them, help them understand things they are exposed to, and, yes, check up on them.

I have to check up on them?

Children need to learn responsible action. Learning responsible action requires having someone checking up on you. You can't check up on someone who has absolute privacy.

Think about it in the physical world. Don't you look in their rooms to see if they've cleaned it? Don't you check to see if they actually took out the trash? Don't you talk to their teachers to see how they are doing in school? Of course you do all those things. It's the only way for them to learn to be responsible. If your child had absolute privacy, you wouldn't have the access or the ability to check any of those things.

Limited privacy is your children being able to shut the door of their rooms in your house to be alone when they need to be. Children having unlimited control of their own passwords isn't like that at all. That's absolute privacy. It's comparable to them living alone in an apartment that you aren't allowed to visit, in a city 10 times the size of yours. If they aren't old enough to legally live alone, they don't need that kind of privacy.

What's the worst that can happen?

Perhaps some parents are naive enough to believe that the worst that can happen is their children might see some inappropriate content or be exposed to intense profanity. But real-life dangers exist out there in the world, and the internet is one way for them to enter your home.

If you don't know your child's passwords, there's no way to trace what has happened if they get in trouble. If your child goes missing, the answer to what happened could be hidden behind their passwords. The same goes with a potential cyberbullying incident involving social media. The worst thing that can happen if you don't know your child's passwords isn't pornography. It is that you may be powerless to help them when something goes wrong.

Once you know the passwords, protect them

You need to protect passwords better than you currently are. Because your children already know your passwords. Are you wondering how we can say that? Well, several reasons.

First, most people are really terrible when it comes to making strong passwords. So, it's a good guess that your passwords are terrible. Some of your passwords are just "password." Some of you use "0000" as your unlock code on your phone because it's the easiest code to type. And most of you probably also use the same password for all your accounts. To get into your bank, your Netflix© account, your email, your tax returns or anything else, you use the same password. That's not a great idea. But a lot of us do it. This doesn't just make it easy for criminals to ruin your life, it makes it easy for your children to ruin theirs.

The other reason we know your kids have figured out your password is that most children are quicker than you, are smarter than you think they are, see better than you do, and have a better memory. So, guess what? You basically live in a house with tiny super spies who can see you tap on the screen from across the room and learn your unlock code for your phone. They can easily figure out that your password to the computer is their birthday. They watch you and know what code you put in to unlock Netflix.

We've even known children who have their parent's thumbprints on a piece of tape or paper that they use to unlock thumbprint-protected devices like iPhones. Don't underestimate them — your children are brilliant! To stop them, you'll need to up your game, get some help, and be vigilant.

An old-school way that still works

One of the best ways to up your game is old-school: Use a password-protected spreadsheet. Put a password-protected spreadsheet on your computer. Choose a good password to protect it, and change that password often! Then enter in all your children's accounts and their passwords. You can keep your passwords in the same document if you want to, or use a different document. This method does require a good bit of work for you to maintain it, but it is simple and doesn't cost anything other than the effort and time you put into it. For an extra level of security, instead of putting the password-protected spreadsheet on your computer, put it on a password-protected thumbdrive, with a different password, and keep the thumb drive on your keys.

Get help if you need it

The other way is to use an app or password service. There are a lot of very good ones out there. We'd love to recommend one to you here, but the way technology changes, it's probably better for you to check some online reviews and choose one that you think will work the best for you. Remember, you want it to store and keep your passwords safe from your children as well as store and keep their passwords so that you will have access. I (Titania) use both the old-school way as well as LastPass. As of date of publication, LastPass (https://www.lastpass.com/) is the top-rated and most secure password manager.

Stay vigilant

Once you have the passwords, all you have to do is check in on some kind of schedule. Check at least once a week to make sure that they haven't changed the password to lock you out. Some accounts, such as social media accounts, may have the option of notifying you via email before allowing a password change. Make sure the email for that setting is an email account your children don't have access to and that you will notice when the notification comes in.

You don't have to watch every move they make. Just check in periodically and let them know that you have been checking in. Do this the way you should be doing everything else in your relationship: by engaging them in conversation. Ask questions about things, give input, and congratulate them on good choices you notice. Remember, you aren't spying on them. You are walking with them through a dangerous area, training them to be responsible and aware of their surroundings. Treat this just like any other normal part of your relationship. Your children's passwords should be like their friends. You should know them.

Passwords are just the beginning of keeping your children safe and training them to live with technology. Passwords simply open up devices, files, services, and apps. Once those doors are open, there are many more settings and limits you need to set up. Therefore, when we add technology to our homes, we need to do it in a careful way.

CHAPTER 14

THE NEW +
WHAT TO DO

When you add something new to your home, it brings a whole series of changes. New technology brings new possibilities. Some of those possibilities are benefits — time savings, new services, access to new information, or new capabilities. But some of those possibilities include new dangers as well.

New hardware? Opt in to parental controls

Getting new technology ready for your children

New stuff is awesome. Everyone loves getting new stuff. And one of the top things we love about new stuff is unwrapping it and starting to use it for the very first time. There is even a bizarre genre of videos on the internet of people "unboxing" subscription boxes, toy boxes, gadget boxes, and all manner of new technology products — "oohing" and "ahhing" over the sleekness of packaging and the presentation of the items inside.

However, if you are in the U.S. when you add new hardware to your home, it will not be ready for your children to use it right out of the box. Every new item will have unique parental controls that have to be activated first. That is because in the U.S., we are automatically opted in for mature content in most cases. In many places around the world, mature content is automatically opted out, often at the internet service provider level. That means that in those countries, when you sign up for internet service or buy new technology, mature content is automatically blocked and you have to opt in to access mature content. Here, that is not the case. Everything you buy will automatically be open to any and all content. If you want to restrict access to mature content, you need to opt out of it via the parental controls built into the technology. That's why, before you give your children the new tablet or the new game system, or any new technology item, you need to set up the parental controls ahead of time.

Yes, this does mean that you'll need to open it first. Open the box, cut open the packaging, turn the device on, read the instructions about setting up the parental controls, adjust the settings, and set the passwords. Depending on the device, this can take a while, so don't try to do this five minutes before your child's birthday party. Give yourself plenty of time to play with it, learn the controls, and familiarize yourself with the settings — especially if it's a device you have never used before. Then, make sure it is completely charged up, put it back in the packaging, tape it up, wrap it up, and give it to your child.

Your child won't get the "unboxing" experience. But that's a minor pleasure compared to opening it up and being instantly ready to start playing with it. Imagine yourself coming in to see your presents on Christmas morning. Would you be happy to see a box full of steel tubing, nuts, bolts, gears, handlebars, and wheels? Or would you prefer to see a fully assembled bike, ready to ride with training wheels attached?

New technology hardware comes with "some assembly required." If you give your daughter an iPod Touch right out of the box, she'll get to open it, but then you'll just have to take it away for a couple hours to set up all the controls. That's not a happy solution. Your children won't care much that a box has been opened or the packaging is not perfect. When they realize that you took the time to set something up for them so that they can use it immediately, they will love you for it. Opening up fully charged, ready-to-use technology is way more fun than opening a box with all the manufacturer's seals still in place.

New software? "Buy" one, get one

Adding apps one at a time
Adding a new piece of hardware isn't the end. New functionality and possibilities are opened with every single app or piece of software that you allow your children to install on their devices. If you open the floodgates and let them add whatever they want, whenever they want, you are going to run into trouble.

Instead, go slowly. Choose carefully. **Add one app at a time and learn each new app along with them**. Once they have demonstrated they are trustworthy with the one, they can add one more. They may protest, but remember that their excuses are just that: excuses.

Remember your purpose — you're training them to be independent. You have to work with them, show them, and teach them how and why to use each app. This is true of almost any app, but it's doubly true about social media.

Social media
For the sake of this discussion, let's just assume that your children are over 13. If you're going to let them join a social media platform, make sure you

decide carefully which one it'll be. Consider the different strengths of the platforms, how many friends are using each one, and what the purpose is for the platform. Then, join the platform together.

Understand how it functions

Social networks have similarities and differences. They aren't all alike. You and your child need to explore and learn how the platform works. How do you choose who you are connected to? How do you control who sees your posts? How do you see your friends' posts? Does this reveal your location and if so, how do you control that? Can you edit a post? Can you delete one? How do you block spam accounts or accounts sharing inappropriate content? Can anyone on the platform send you a direct message or chat with you, or just your connections? Understanding all of these features takes some getting used to and some investigation. Use the question, "Can you teach me?"

What is its purpose?

Every social network has a purpose for why it exists or a question that it is asking. Participation in a social media platform means trying to answer that question and contributing to its purpose. Use the question, "What do you think about [platform's certain feature]?" to foster communication around the means the platform uses to fulfill its purpose.

As you learn about your child's perception of a platform and what it can do, use your influence to shape that perception into a useful interaction with the platform. Every app developer has a purpose for the platform they're building. With their apps, developers are answering questions, and it's our responsibility to understand a platform's purpose and the questions that it is answering. From there, train your child as to the purpose of the platform, and how your child can participate in executing that purpose in the right ways.

For example, the concise purpose of Instagram is to share photos and videos with other people online. Asking your child how they would like to participate in that purpose opens communication. Your child might answer you with, "Well, I want to post things that will get a lot of likes from my friends." This is where you help them understand the right way to achieve likes — by providing help to friends. If your child is in a band, on a gymnastics team or plays soccer, they could very easily take pictures of gear and share reviews on Instagram. Or they could take videos of practices. They could follow Instagram users with similar interests and ask questions. Imagine if your son or daughter followed Ezequiel Barco (MLS soccer player for Atlanta United) and reached out to ask him a question: "When you were growing up, what was your favorite soccer skill to learn, and how did you master it?" And imagine that Barco replied. Your child could repost Barco's answer to his or her Instagram account, tagging Barco, tagging Atlanta United, and using appropriate hashtags to share knowledge from a professional.

Teaching your child the purpose of each platform, and how to appropriately use a platform — one platform at a time — is your number one job as your family's director of information technology. When your child knows and understands a platform's purpose, using curiosity in the right ways — something you teach them how to do — allows your child to build trust with you as they use the platform in ways that support and grow that purpose.

Build trust and learn responsibility

Just like they do in any other area of life, children need to build trust so that they understand what to do and what not to do. They need to show responsibility in the way they use the new platform. On any social network (or even just with texting) you can't hold your children responsible for what someone else sends, or shares to them, or comments, but you can hold them responsible for how they respond.

Children build trust in this area just like they would when learning to drive a car. They start as a learner and you have to do it with them. Next they prove through guided experience that they have gained a level of skill and competence. Then, they prove that they can be trusted to continue to operate the vehicle without you present. That's how learning something works. Finally, once they complete this cycle, you can consider what new app or platform they want to add.

You will learn about each other as you learn about the apps
Use the platform you choose to explore their interests. Most social media platforms have search features that let you follow leaders in certain topics. (Note: these search features also let you stumble upon all kinds of inappropriate and graphic content, so be prepared). Does your child like space exploration? Tennis? Dance? Great! Help your children find leaders in those areas to follow. You should follow those leaders, too.

You should have an account on any platform your children do. Follow your children and anyone your children follow. You shouldn't comment or react to everything your children do online, but it's important to be one of their connections. Watch who they follow and who follows them. It won't be long before they follow someone that they probably shouldn't follow or some other questionable activity shows up. When that happens, don't freak out. Have a conversation about it. Use the questions: "Did you see [fill in the blank]? What did you think about that?"

When you move into social media alongside your children, it is simply a way to continue growing your relationship as you model appropriate behavior for them.

Gaming and chat
While talking about apps, we also need to talk about an often forgotten or ignored aspect of gaming: chat. Just about every game has some kind of chat

or messaging feature. Whether your children play games on phones, tablets, handheld game systems, consoles, or computers, they are probably playing a game with a chat feature. Games of all levels — even those for very young children and those with mature content — can have chat. Chat, however, is not rated at all. It is open communication and whoever is on there can say anything that they want. Some games' chat features include direct private messaging between players. The most common problems to pop up on gaming chat will be abusive language and bullying, but there is also the possibility of being enticed to meet up with someone in real life (IRL). You can imagine the myriad dangers possible in that scenario, the least harmful of which is an online fight becoming a real world fight.

Most chat functions in games (and on social media, as well) have some method of reporting offensive or dangerous chat behavior and methods of blocking users who engage in this behavior, but you have to know about that behavior in order to teach your child to report such individuals and to block them. This is another reason to learn and use one app at a time and explore apps with your children. Remember, it's not the technology that makes the bullies and abusers — it just helps facilitate and exacerbate their behavior. Bullies and predators are already out there, and your children could run into them in a hundred different scenarios. The relationship that you build with your children, the questions you ask, and the conversations you invest in are the things that will make the difference in how your children deal with these situations.

When your children encounter bullies or abusive individuals — whether online or IRL — it becomes an opportunity to have conversations about how we treat others, how to forgive, and how to live in a world where people may try to hurt us. Dealing with bullies and difficult people is something your children must learn to do in every aspect of their lives. You wouldn't let them learn about this without any help in real life. Don't leave them alone in the digital world, either.

Just, no

Some apps you should just say "no" to

There are definitely some apps you just need to avoid. If we were speaking in front of a group of people, we would be able to give you a list of apps to avoid and watch out for, but any list we put here will quickly grow less and less useful as more apps are published each day.

So, instead of giving you a list that will be nearly instantly outdated, we're going to recommend a website to help you keep current on what is out there now. We'll also share four dangerous features to watch out for that will tip you off to a potentially bad app.

ProtectYoungEyes.com

For current info about apps and help setting up parental controls on current devices, we recommend checking in regularly at ProtectYoungEyes.com.[17] They do a great job of keeping parents up to date with the latest info about shady apps and things to avoid.

What to ask

When looking at an app, there are two questions that are important to ask before installing the app on your child's phone — we talked about these apps earlier. Ask: "What will it do for me?" and "What can it do?"

Also, ask yourself if this app is set up to help you do things — either online or in real life — that you shouldn't be doing. There are four types of features that, as a rule of thumb, are a dead giveaway that an app is slanted toward illicit purposes. If an app has any of these four features, skip it.

---

17   https://protectyoungeyes.com/

Concealment

Any app that has the purpose of helping you conceal things is bad. Specifically, there are several apps to help you hide photos, screenshots of conversations, and other apps. Most of these function by making a hidden folder on the device that can only be accessed through the app that installed it. Users hide suspicious apps in the hidden folder so that at a glance it doesn't look like there is anything on the device that shouldn't be there. Quick tip: if your child has more than one calculator app on their phone, that's a dead giveaway that one of them is actually a "vault" app that requires a passcode to unlock its contents.

Anonymity

If an app is promising anonymity, it usually isn't for a good reason. Also, if you read the End User License Agreement (EULA), you'll notice that the app can't really promise to keep your data anonymous. Location data, user identification numbers, device type, phone numbers, emails, and other data is collected and can easily be exposed by hackers. Data can also change hands if the company is sold or goes out of business and another company buys the data for its own use. But none of that has to happen for this feature to cause trouble. A lot of trouble, embarrassment, and pain can come about when someone figures out your child is the one who "anonymously" asked a really embarrassing question or revealed something mortifying.

Location-based chatting

A key feature that gives away an app usually used for illicit meetings is location-based chatting. If an app allows you to view people who are online nearby and choose to chat with them, there is not much good that can come of it.

Disappearing messages or photos

You almost certainly want to avoid any app promising to make communication untraceable or invisible. Apps where messages, photos, or videos "disappear" after being seen are usually not places where healthy messages of encouragement are shared. Bullying, sexting, and verbal abuse are common among teens on these platforms. Also, as with the promised "anonymity" in other apps, no picture, text, or video sent between devices is ever truly gone. Nothing on the web disappears. It can be captured on the other person's device as a screenshot and then shared publicly, or it can be hacked or inadvertently released from the company's servers.

Technology isn't risk-free because the world isn't risk-free. Even with the most vigilant parents, the world isn't worry-free, and children can still get hurt through technology.

CHAPTER 15

IT TAKES A VILLAGE

By now, you likely have realized that you can't take on this technology, social media, digital life, online world monitoring role for your family alone. From teachers to grandparents to stepparents to neighbors, there are many people your child has a relationship with and who are capable of helping kids navigate this digital age.

The Facebook group Parenting in a Tech World[18] was created to help parents navigate the ever-changing landscape of raising kids in the digital age. This group provides a much needed space for parents to support each other, get the scoop on cool apps, latest trends, and for all things tech-related.

The group is administered by Bark, a monitoring tool that uses advanced algorithms to alert parents to issues like cyberbullying, sexting, online predation, drug-related content, and signs of depression. But this community isn't just for parents who use Bark — it's for ANY parent raising kids/tweens/teens in a tech world.

---

18   https://www.facebook.com/groups/parentinggeeks

We're the first generation of parents to have kids with smartphones and unsurpassed access to technology. Supporting them while also keeping them safe isn't easy. Reach out, learn, and feel confident that you're helping them navigate through uncharted territory. It takes a village, and this group is a helpful resource in that regard.

When parents come together to support each other, powerful things can happen in the lives of families and children. Here are a handful of examples of the type of community you'll find in the Parenting in a Tech World Facebook Group. (Names have been changed to ensure privacy and content has been edited for clarity.)

Found plans to drink

"I found out my 13-year-old's friends are planning to drink when they all go on a trip later this week. I'm not sure if my daughter's planning to drink, but I'm not going to let her go. How do I discuss this with her? I'm worried she'll find some other way to sneak around." — Bethany B.

> **Comments:**
>
> "I taught my daughter to give the universal reason kids accept: 'My Mom would kill me, and I'd be grounded for months.' I also had an agreement with her that if she was ever somewhere that she didn't feel comfortable, I would pick her up, without any consequences." — Christina J.
>
> "I'd tell her, 'I need you to help me understand.' That way you're putting the ball in her court. Explain what could happen if she drinks. Like you, I wouldn't let her go, but I would offer another option like a sleepover at your house with a friend you can trust." — Jamie T.
>
> "Ask her what she wants and what she thinks is right. Talk to her without judgement, and ask her what she thinks. Remind her that

you have rules but you will always love her. My son's friends started trying alcohol at about the ages of 13 and 14. A parent usually supplied it, although they never admitted it. My son came to me, told me and had questions. I didn't act alarmed or forbid him from talking to his friends — these kids weren't new, my son grew up along with these kids. Also, I was glad he knew he could ask me questions like this. I had an honest talk about it — if he felt pressured to try alcohol, if it was something he thought he would cave into, and I asked him how I could help. He did feel pressured but didn't know how to tell his friends 'No' and still be perceived as 'normal' or 'cool.' With some reassurance from his dad and me, along with reminding him we loved him no matter what, he made good choices and stayed honest with us. He lost his friends, it's been hard, but he didn't give in and he did it his way (not ours)." — Cortney P.

Rules for visitors

"What type of rules do you have at your house when your kids' friends come over and bring their phones? (Ages 12-15)" — Angela M.

Comments:

"After our eye opening experiences anyone who comes into our home now has their phones put in the safe. If their folks need to talk to them, they just text me and I'll get them their phone and put it back when they're done. No cells, no smart devices, no tablets, not even a kindle! But the kids know it before they come over and they still come, so it can't be that bad." — Mis L.

"No phones during meals, and at 9 p.m. we take all devices. Kids and parents know the rules beforehand. All parents have thanked me for it. The kids get it back in the morning; parents know to text me if they need to. I will say, when the screens disappear, that's when the laughter truly erupts from the basement. They actually have fun like the good old days. My oldest daughter, 12, prefers technology-free sleepovers." — Stella C.

"We've worked hard at having good relationships with 13- and 15-year-old sons' friends. They know our rules and we know theirs. Our boys and the friends turn the phones in at night, no questions asked. The friends' parents are supportive because they know without question we love their kids like our own and we know they love our boys. We also don't allow doors closed when screens are in their possession. It's possible, there have been a couple boys struggle at first but the core group of boys love being together, and we do everything we can to help them have fun and feel comfortable. We don't act rigid or controlling about it. Just matter of fact, and some donut bribery the first couple times if they are new — and occasionally the old timers too. Your kid has to be all onboard too and not act annoyed. We often have three to six soccer teammates over on any weekend. Make it not a big deal and it usually isn't. Involve food if it's boys." — Holly G.

Adult friend won't go away

"Please, I need help. This is going to be long, but I'm at a loss. Instagram: I have an account to follow my 16-year-old daughter and some of her friends. I also have full access to log into hers to see what she's actually doing. She friended a guy that lives in another state about six months ago. (This was not the first time but others were her age and are now gone. This one is different.) I have tried talking to her about if this is who he really is. He is a 20-year-old college student, so he says, and, in my opinion, very needy, depressed, lonely (by his own making) and immature. I decided to start following him a few months ago to see how she would handle this and to "know" him. He knows I follow him and so does she. My daughter insists he is one of her best friends. I have messaged him two times in these months asking him to limit his interactions and to gradually go away from her — and to keep this between him and I as adults... to be the grown-up, he hasn't. The first time he told her that I had contacted him, and it made her upset but no major meltdown. The second time, he told her again, and said that he's got to be careful but no reason as to why. So my daughter assumed he was thinking because of his age and not because of me messaging him. The two weeks following that second text were great and even she seemed more upbeat. Well, he has forgotten about both those messages apparently. Four days ago, when I did a check on her account, I found they had sent each other pictures. I don't know what of because they disappear after being seen. I pray they were innocent as the conversation was about Christmas. I did another check this morning and saw videos and pics went back and forth again throughout last evening. He is very negative and dark in his posts and even in his DMs with her. I have noticed that when she talks with him, she becomes sad and seems like she takes on his negativity. Recently, she said he wants to visit her here for her birthday in the spring. Ummm, no. Yes, she does tell me what they talk about, but I still check occasionally just to be sure because of his age and being on the other side of the country. I need him gone yet not lose the openness I have with my daughter. She will not unfollow or block him, I already know that as she insists he needs her as she is his only 'positive friend.' No, I do not want to take her Instagram account away because other than this one person, she is doing alright and improving with it overall. I've thought about messaging him again, pretending to be her dad wondering if he'd listen more. Help!" — Susan K.

Comments:

"She is being groomed. I can't tell you what to do but my now 16-year-old could — she was groomed and believed, and she was harmed in ways I won't list here. She happened to be stealing phones or having people buy them for her to communicate on Instagram and Snapchat. SHUT HIM DOWN legally and do it now. Protect her like you would if a creep came to your door. Lock the windows and doors to technology and get her in therapy so she can talk about what she HASN'T told you yet." — Andrea M.

"My kids and I have an agreement that they only follow people that they have met in person, and if they saw them in person they would say, 'Hi.' They don't and shouldn't follow everyone in their school and friends of friends, etc. If they abuse this, they know they lose Instagram. It sounds like grooming to me. For him to pay attention to her and then ignore her and say he wants to come meet her is scary. He's playing games, and he knows you are involved and doesn't care. I'm sorry you are dealing with this and it sounds like there isn't a good way to get out now without causing issues between the two of you but you should listen to your gut and do what is safest." — Rochelle P.

Update: Susan K. reported him from her account and her daughter's account.

First smartphone

"At what age did your kids get their first smartphone? I'm thinking never. Lol. New to this group." — Joan D.

Comments:

"Seventh grade. No social media. Just turned 15 and still no social media and has screen time and text time limits." — Erica C.

"10 yrs (5th grade). Her father and I are separated and we needed a way to communicate while apart." — Samantha D.

"I've joined the Wait for 8th campaign, which is roughly age 14. Lots of research about brain development to support it. So that's what we will do! My middle schooler hates me. Haha!" — Cindy R.

"Age 14, with a 'contract' that had many terms to it!" — Brenda A.

Sexting

"My teen has inappropriate sexual conversations with a girl. Not the first time I've caught him. We are quite isolated from other kids and social media is the tool for communication and keeping in touch with school friends so I don't know if taking his phone away or shutting down social media communications is the answer. I don't actually know how to "control" this behavior. It's obviously in his heart, the conversations just feed the desire so of course I want to put a stop to this. Do I just take away his phone, do I just continue to monitor his conversations? When he is back at school I will limit phone access and social media, but I actually have no idea what to do. Any ideas would be helpful." — Victoria W.

Comments:

"I think I would make sure he understood the legalities of these conversations and know where the line is so it's not crossed. I'd also talk a lot about respect and consent." — Melanie K.

"That's a tough one mama. Lots of kids engage in explicit sexual communication. I've talked to kids who say their behavior online is completely different than in person. There's a couple of things that come to mind here. First, how does he feel about the behavior? Does he see anything inappropriate about it? Remember they are learning how to speak from the internet. Second, does he understand that just because the girl is engaged in the conversation that it doesn't necessarily translate to what the girl wants? You may not be able to control how he acts but he still needs guidance and council from you. Start by acknowledging his feelings. Bring it back to relationships in real life. How do we want to be treated? How do we want to treat others? It may not seem like he's listening. But keep talking as openly as possible. Something will start to sink in. It'll matter that you care." — Marilyn E.

"When I read an inappropriate text my son sent to a friend, I was mortified. It took me two days to calm down and get grounded. Instead of having the conversation at home, I told him we have something important to talk about, and I took him out for a Starbucks. I spoke using 'I statements,' and I shared my own experiences of growing up, as well as how I felt as a mom when I read the text. (He is aware I read/spot check his messages.) We talked about natural sexual curiosity, what were his motivations, how she may feel, and then the consequences of putting our thoughts out to the world — where they can never be taken back. I've never been so proud of the authentic apology he wrote all by himself. I feel this was a tech 'win,' as no adult ever had a conversation like that with me when I was a teen. My heart goes out to you, as you make these parenting decisions, knowing what's best for your family. You've got this!" — Annemarie O.

Why no social media?

"My kiddo and I keep bumping heads about social media apps. He's 13. We've decided no social media apps on phones. He's asking for validation as to why. Besides the fact it's unhealthy (and causes kids so much unnecessary drama), how else do you parents explain this to your young teens? And does anyone have a good article to share? Side note: He is asking if he can at least have Facebook. I don't even understand why because none of his friends have it. It seems he's just looking for some freedom, which I understand. What are the precautions with Facebook that I should be aware of?" — Kim D.

Comments:

"I would take a different approach. Instead of justifying your position to him, have HIM research and give you a 1,000 word research paper — complete with citing valid sources — as to why he should be allowed to have Facebook or some other source of social media.

Now, if you do this, you have to go into it with an open mind that he may succeed in convincing you. If he does, you will agree to a heavily parent-monitored account. My daughter is a ballerina and she does have a parent-monitored Instagram at age 14 for networking and self promotion. However, other than that, you'd be hard pressed to convince me. My son is 12, and he wants social media. As soon as I said to write a 1,000 word research essay, he said, 'I'm out; not worth it!' LOL He doesn't bring it up often, but when he does, I say, 'I haven't seen that research essay yet.'" — Melody F.

"Make him convince you why, not vice versa. That being said, we're going to start with Facebook at 13. It's not the cool choice, but Facebook offers extensive logs of all activity, more control over what you see on your own homepage, and the filtering is so much better than many of the other platforms. Messenger does offer secret messaging but it's kinda hard to find, and it can be turned on and off (and you can tell who has it on if you try to message them). Plus this is where our family is — I would LOVE for my kids to use social media as it's intended, to keep in touch with extended family. I want them to get in the habit of posting for grandma, not posting for likes." — Jessica M.

What happens at 18?

"Sooo... what about the OLDER TEENS? 17-19? My son will be 17 next month. He'll graduate next summer and start community college afterwards. (He will continue to live at home until he transfers.) We have a contract, so he knows that I check his phone whenever I see fit. But what happens when they turn 18? Start paying for their own cells? Does anyone still monitor/control then? Also, GPS still?" — Kathryn F.

Comments:
"My son is 19; he graduates this year. He also plans to live at home

and attend community college. I don't check his phone anymore. I've accepted that at his age, I've taught him well and it is now 100% up to him the kind of person he wants to be. He also knows his choices now have big people consequences. At this stage, it's no longer about me punishing him or policing him, but about him feeling free to talk to me about anything so I can continue to give him my advice, whether he takes it or not." — Megan G.

"Hopefully you have had discussions about your local and state laws, and talked about safety and the internet. We have to trust that as they become adults, they have the capability to manage on their own. Once they turn 18, they are on their own legally, and nothing we can do will stop any legal charges. Prepare them with open discussion, so they are making the right choices. Whether you own the phone or not, they get the legal ramifications of their choices." — Nancy N.

Relating limits for better understanding

"Hey, I just wanted to share a success I had with my kids. My 10-year-old son isn't usually interested in social media stuff, but occasionally he'll ask why we don't do it or why he can't have a phone, etc. I had the thought to show him the scene from *Finding Nemo* where Dory and Marlon are swimming through the jellyfish and then Dory gets stung.

"I told him that I'm Marlon, he's Dory, and the jellyfish are the internet/social media apps, etc. Marlon knows that the jellyfish are dangerous, and he knows how to navigate them without issues, but Dory doesn't know the danger and she's unable to protect herself. And despite doing her best to avoid it, she eventually gets stung and nearly dies. But she wouldn't have been stung if she'd listened to Marlon and stayed above the jellyfish. And then I told my son (and my other kids who were listening) that, 'We're not going into the jellyfish. We are swimming above them where I know you can stay safe until you have the ability to understand the dangers and the capacity to protect yourself. Because when you swim through jellyfish, it's not *if* you get stung but *when*. And when you swim through the internet, it's not *if* something happens, it's *when*.

"That really helped him understand why I have the rules I do, and what my motives are. When the internet world looks like a bunch of trampolines you bounce around on, it's hard to see that you'd get stung by the tentacles. And since he's actually been stung by a jellyfish, he knows how bad it hurts! Anyway, just thought I'd share this in case any of you were looking for a way to explain things to tweens. I totally feel like it was an inspired thought! Not sure I have the capacity to think of that example without some divine assistance!" — Brenna W.

Comments:

"Great analogy! Keep on swimming momma, you're doing a great job." — Karie H.

"Fantastic. So glad you shared. Will save this kid-friendly analogy for our own social media chats and more." — Kelly E.

"Thank you so much for sharing!! This is great and such a developmentally appropriate explanation. Definitely will be using this analogy with my 10- and 9-year-olds as well as my elementary students. I'm a school counselor. Thanks again!" — Susan G.

These are just a few examples of the support, encouragement, and advice that the 90k+ parents in the Parenting in a Tech World Facebook group share on a daily basis.

For some parents, it takes a lot to open up and be vulnerable among their peers. But what can be learned when we share transparently, has the potential to create ripples of ideas and change in families across the world.

It is okay to ask for help. Find a supportive community that reflects your values and open up to them. Your stories and your insights will be valuable to other parents on their journey.

CHAPTER 16

GOOD DIGITAL CITIZEN

Throughout these chapters, we've emphasized that you're raising children in a complex technological, social media-driven world. Educating, enabling, riding beside, and setting boundaries is how you teach a child to "fish," or use social media, for a lifetime. None of us intend to plop a super-computer into our child's lap at 13 and expect them to be able to navigate the nuances of communication or relationships in the online world.

A technology contract is a great way for your family to collaborate on rules for using devices and accessing the internet. It can help make sure the whole family is on the same page about how to get the most out of technology, and — most importantly — how to stay safer online.

This is a tech contract template Bark created that lists a few agreements we think are important, plus a few spaces to add your own limits or agreements you'd like to make with your children. A free, downloadable version is available at www.bark.us.

CHILD & PARENT
TECH CONTRACT

I will:

☐ Immediately answer a call or text from my mom, dad, or other family member.

☐ Ask my parents before I download any apps on my phone.

☐ Ask my parents before sharing any photos online.

☐ Tell an adult if anything online makes me nervous or afraid.

☐ Leave my phone in the kitchen to charge at night.

☐ _____

☐ _____

☐ _____

☐ _____

I will not:

☐ Share my address, phone number, or other personal information online.

☐ Add, text, or interact with anyone online that I do not know.

☐ Be mean, spread rumors, or make fun of people online.

☐ Make fake profiles or pretend to be someone else on the internet.

☐ Use my phone during school unless there is an emergency.

☐ Use my phone (calls, text, or social) while I am driving.

☐ _____

☐ _____

☐ _____

I understand that:

☐ My parents can take my phone away from me at any time.

☐ Having a phone is a responsibility that I will take seriously.

☐ _____

☐ _____

Child Signature - - - - - - - - - - - - - - - - - -

Parent Signature - - - - - - - - - - - - - - - - - -

bark
www.bark.us

Bark helps keep kids safe online and in real life.

Consider a technology contract as collateral for your child's device

As more and more kids have access to connected devices, the pressure for parents to provide kids with their own smartphones and tablets is heating up. But technology is a privilege, not a right. In most cases, parents are the owners of their kids' devices, not the kids themselves. It's okay to remind your kids that you're loaning them the device in good faith, and for you require them to sign a technology contract in exchange.

Set the ground rules

While the internet offers amazing possibilities, there are also many dangers that exist online. Here are a few points to consider:

- For younger kids, we recommend setting their password for any and all accounts they access, and to make sure your child isn't allowed to change them. If your child is older, you may want to consider letting them set their own passwords. With either approach, including a monitoring tool like Bark will provide an extra layer of safety to their online activity.

- It's your right as a parent to look through the device at any point to see which sites they visit and who they're communicating with online.

- Make sure your child knows to never video chat with strangers, and that they're not allowed to provide any personal information on any forum or website without your permission. This includes their name, address, school, birthday, or any other information a stranger could use to find them.

- For teens with a driver's license, make sure you have a strict no-texting-while-driving rule in place. This is not only the law in many states — it's also practical advice that can help keep your kids safe on the road. Check out AT&T's It Can Wait[19] campaign. It's raising awareness of distracted driving and encouraging teens to put their phones down whenever they're behind the wheel.

---

19   https://www.itcanwait.com/

- Make it clear that there are consequences for breaking the terms of the technology contract. Consequences can include the loss of privileges associated with their device, losing access to the device for a set time period, or anything else that makes sense for your family.
- Remind your child that you're a team that's in this together. Mistakes will happen, but you're there to discuss anything with them so you can learn and grow together.

Discuss online etiquette

In addition to setting safety rules for your child, you'll also want to help them understand that there is a basic etiquette for navigating the online world. For example, you could set rules about turning the device off in certain public places like restaurants or at the movies. Or consider rules where the whole family puts their devices away during dinner or leaves them in the kitchen to charge overnight while sleeping.

Your child may know how to be a good person in real life, but the anonymity of the internet can sometimes blur the lines. It's a good idea to clearly spell out that they should never lie to people online. Remind your child to be a good friend who never promotes or shares hurtful messaging, either. If your child is old enough to access social media sites, teach them the basics of privacy. And if you're using Bark, explain that you're monitoring their activity to ensure their safety (much like you urge them to wear a bicycle helmet or apply sunscreen), not to snoop.

Model the behavior you want your child to emulate

Children watch what the adults in their lives are doing, so be mindful of how you use technology around them. For example, a "no smartphone at the dinner table" rule should include adults, too. Set a good example and interact with technology in the same manner you expect from your child. The internet opens doors to amazing things for your child, and the conversation around responsibility, respect, and safety should be ongoing as technology continues to evolve. With a technology contract in place, everyone in the family can refer to it for clear expectations and actions.

Monitor your kid's activities

In addition to setting up a tech contract as a family and having regular conversations about internet safety, you can use Bark to monitor your child's online activities. Even after talking about your family's rules about the internet, your child might not always follow them. That's why having an additional safeguard in place can be helpful.

Our award-winning monitoring service alerts parents and guardians when there's a potential issue they need to know about — including cyberbullying, sexting, online predators, depression, suicidal thoughts, threats of violence, and more. Sign up today at Bark.us to monitor your child's texts, email, YouTube, and 30+ apps and social media platforms, and get one week of our service completely free.

CHAPTER 17

BE ON THE LOOKOUT

If you watch police procedurals (and if you watch TV at all, it's hard to escape them), you have probably heard this acronym: BOLO. It's one of those bits of jargon that washes over us, and we kind of get what it means from context, but many people don't know what it actually stands for — be on the lookout. As a parent, you aren't on the lookout for dangerous suspects, but for changes that can indicate that there is a problem to investigate.

There are two main areas to watch for changes. One is **relational** — looking for changes in the behavior of your children and family members. One is **technical** — looking for changes in settings, usage, and data that affect your family.

Relational markers — online affects offline

People often behave in incredibly different ways online than they do in real life. Some of the meekest, most polite children can be the meanest, most ruthless bullies online. As far as your children are concerned, the online world and the real world are one and the same. They don't experience them as separate places, and though their behavior may be different, the emotional effects can carry over from one to the other and cause noticeable changes.

Know your family

My hope for you is that you know your family members well. You have to know them well in order to know when something is wrong. If you aren't well attuned to what's normal, you won't be able to spot fluctuating signals.

Changes

At the most basic level, you are looking for changes. Below is a list of some areas to watch. Sudden changes in these areas are warning signs that something may be going on.

- Moods/emotional outbursts
- School performance
- Behavior problems
- Obsession with secrecy/privacy
- Shutting down/not participating in school or family activities anymore
- Appetite changes

Allies

A BOLO is a call for help from allies in law enforcement. Similarly, you can't be everywhere your child goes or see your child in every situation. You need to have some allies to help you spot some of these signs. Most of us aren't with our children all the time and, even if you are, you need an outside perspective to see things you might miss. Here is a list of some common allies who may be able to give you valuable information about your children's lives.

- Relatives
- School teachers or administrators
- Church small group leaders
- Coaches

- Tutors
- Instructors in dance, music, or the arts.
- Spouses (Including ex-spouses and their new spouses)
- Friends (Both your friends and your children's friends)

Check in with your allies regularly. Have conversations and ask questions about your children.

- What have you seen in my children that was interesting? Surprised you? Scared you? Made you laugh?
- What's the craziest thing my children are doing? You've heard? You've seen?
- Can you teach me how...?

You need to listen proactively to people who interact with your children and learn from their perspective. Sometimes you learn more about your children from their behavior when you're not around than when you are. Invest in having a good relationship and regular communication with these allies. This gives you another window into your children's world and will multiply your chances of getting an early warning of problems in their lives.

Technical markers — monitoring the data

It's very helpful to monitor and check in on some usage data that can help you spot potential issues. Here are a few areas that you can check periodically on your own to get a better idea of what's going on in your child's world. To make things easier, you can also use a service or hardware to monitor some of these areas for you.

- Data usage — If data usage has a huge spike, more than normal, you know that a big change has happened in how much information is coming into your home. What is causing that spike in data? Music? Movies? Pictures?
- Internet browsing history — You should check your browsing history periodically. (If you are using a browser that users log in to, like Google

Chrome, then you will need to log in as your children in order to check theirs.) If you notice that a day or week of browser history is deleted, someone may be hiding something.

- Network slow downs — Your network can slow down when large amounts of data are being downloaded or uploaded. It can also happen when you have hardware that blocks access to some content. When someone is trying to access restricted content, the device blocks that access and that can cause your network to slow down.

You can monitor these things on your own or you can find a service or device that will do it for you. The service I (Matt) use recently flagged some activity that I then had to investigate.

We have a basement apartment in our home that we rented out to a young intern from a local church. He was a great guy — taking classes and pursuing a career in ministry. I loved that my children had a big brother now, who sort of lived with us. But after he moved in, I saw some markers, some red flags. My network was dragging way down. When I checked the monitoring device I saw why. It was blocking a BitTorrent server that was running on our network.

If you don't know what that is, it's a file-sharing protocol. It allows people to share really large files. It has a lot of legitimate uses, but has also been used for some shady things, like movie piracy and mature content. That's why the monitoring device was set to block access.

I see a marker. Now what?

It all comes back to conversation and relationships. It doesn't matter if you spot a technical marker or a relational marker, the reaction should be the same. Use questions to engage in conversation. Your aim is to investigate the change — the marker — not your child.

In the situation I just described, it was a technical marker that came up, and I found myself having a conversation with a young man, who's not my child, about internet usage. I had to talk with him and work out what was going on. He was using the torrent for a school project. Nothing bad. But I still had to have the conversation.

In the story about my son in the introduction, it was an emotional marker that caused me to ask the right kind of question to my son. The answer to that question led to a conversation that saved my son and my family further damage.

Being on the lookout for relational and technical changes is just the beginning. It's an indicator of a possible problem. The way you find out if there actually is a problem — and the way you solve the problem if one is there — is through questions that lead to conversations that build your relationship, just as we discussed in previous chapters.

When your child needs help

Unfortunately, there may be a time when your child needs more than your guidance to navigate a problem or situation that is at the root of their emotional changes. If you suspect your child needs professional assistance, reach out to any of these national help lines:

National Suicide Hotline
Available 24/7
Helps individuals in suicidal crisis with support
1-800-273-8255
https://suicidepreventionlifeline.org

Child Help USA National Hotline

Available 24/7, in over 170 languages

Helps youth who are suffering child abuse

1-800-4-A-CHILD (1-800-422-4453)

http://www.childhelpusa.org/

Crisis Textline

Available 24/7

Support to all individuals in crisis

Text "HELLO" to 741741

www.crisistextline.org

Trevor Project Lifeline

Available 24/7

Confidential suicide hotline for LGBT youth

866-488-7386

http://www.thetrevorproject.org

Boys Town National Hotline

Available 24/7

Serving all at-risk teens and children

Call: 800-448-3000

http://www.boystown.org/hotline/

Substance Abuse Mental Health Awareness National Helpline

24/7, English and Spanish

Support and referral for drug and alcohol services

1-800-662-HELP (4357)

https://www.samhsa.gov/find-help/national-helpline

National Teen Dating Violence Hotline

Available 24/7

Questions or concerns about dating relationships

1-866-331-9474

Text "loveis" to 22522

http://www.loveisrespect.org

National Eating Disorders Helpline

Available Mon.–Thurs. 9:00 a.m.–9:00 p.m., Fri.9:00 a.m.–5:00 p.m. (EST)

Support, resources, and treatment options for people struggling with eating disorders

Hotline 1-800-931-2237

www.nationaleatingdisorders.org

National Sexual Assault Hotline

Available 24/7

Supports victims of sexual assault, LGBT-inclusive

1-800-656-HOPE 24/7 or

Online Counseling at www.rainn.org

CHAPTER 18

HELP ME, I DON'T "DO" TECH

The farther along the technology journey, the less anyone, young or old, can use the excuse that they don't "do" tech. Even the Silent Generation — the parents of Boomers — are learning technology to stay in touch with children and grandchildren across the country. Simple controls on the latest smartphones help these older generations to use FaceTime and chat.

We've talked before about how ignorance isn't an excuse. What's at stake — your child's safety, innocence, reputation, and even their life — is so much more important than the discomfort and confusion you might feel for a while as you learn technology.

Think about this: Every older generation has had to learn new technology. New devices for communicating, new methods of transportation, new machines to make their jobs easier. Even if they were familiar with computers when computers were first introduced, when the implementation of updated software arrived, they had to learn updated or new programs.

Just think what it was like for our parents the first time they ordered cable TV, picked up the remote, and stumbled upon Cinemax and HBO. Whoa! Not only did the content of these cable networks push the envelope, the formatting and production techniques changed. Lighting techniques changed, bringing drama and intrigue. Even music scores became more interlaced with lighting and camera work as just one more element to fascinate us and hold our attention.

The same thing is happening in social media. Every platform has some type of "discovery" section, where users can browse content that is similar to — but slightly different from — the content they're currently consuming in the app. Some of that content in the discovery section might push your child into questionable content. Don't you want to know how to help your child navigate that when it happens? Don't you want to spare them anxiety, depression, harassment, and possibly emotional and physical wounds? Without the guidance from their parents or guardians, kids may stumble down the wrong path. Being flippant and proclaiming that you don't "do" tech is not good enough for your child's well-being.

Earlier generations adapted and increased their skillset despite the discomfort of learning something unfamiliar. Undoubtedly, there are people who believe they can develop their intelligence about social media and technology, and there are those who think they can't or that they will fail. The way these two types of people operate can be described as exercising either a growth mindset or a fixed mindset.

Growth mindset

Author Carol Dweck defines a growth mindset this way: "In a growth mindset, people believe that their most basic abilities can be developed through dedication and hard work — brains and talent are just the starting point. This view creates a love of learning and a resilience that is essential for great accomplishment."[20]

People with a growth mindset believe that intelligence can be developed, which leads to a love of learning and a tendency to embrace challenges, persist despite obstacles, see effort as a path to mastery, learn from criticism, and be inspired by others' success.

Fixed mindset

In contrast, Dweck defines a fixed mindset as: "In a fixed mindset, people believe their basic qualities, like their intelligence or talent, are simply fixed traits. They spend their time documenting their intelligence or talent instead of developing them. They also believe that talent alone creates success — without effort."

Those with this type of mindset believe intelligence is fixed. This leads to a tendency to try and "look smart," which leads to performance-based behavior. People with a fixed mindset have a tendency to avoid challenges, give up easily due to obstacles, see effort as fruitless, ignore useful feedback, and be threatened by others' success.

Which one are you?

We would predict that most people who say they don't "do" tech are people who have a fixed mindset. Maybe they don't believe they will "get it." If you identify with the descriptions of a person with a fixed mindset, there are things you can do to start moving in a different direction.

First of all, believe that you can change. Just the mere thought of, "I can change," or "I can learn this," begins to change the wiring in your brain to being more open to adapting. What we think of ourselves and of our

---

20   https://www.renaissance.com/edwords/growth-mindset/

abilities, tend to bring about our reality — more often than we'd like.

Second, there are some practical ways you can begin to take care of your brain and move toward the growth mindset belief that intelligence can be developed. These practical ways include: exercising, meditating, mental exercise (think crossword puzzles), reducing sugar, reducing caffeine, reducing alcohol, making note of what you enjoy about life more than what you don't enjoy, and getting good sleep.

You can learn technology and social media

Because of today's technology, we have access to substantial libraries of information, video tutorials, and online classes about any subject matter you choose, including social media apps, gaming systems, and smart devices. From 2-minute overviews to 15-minute, step-by-step video directions, you can find the training and information you need to stay engaged with technology and ultimately with your child as they navigate this online world.

Some tutorial resources to consider:

Udemy.com — By connecting students all over the world to the best instructors, we are helping individuals reach their goals and pursue their dreams. (Classes on various subjects.)

Skillshare.com — We want to inspire and multiply the kind of creative exploration that furthers expression, learning and application. (Classes on various subjects.)

Linkedin.com/learning — We administer personalized learning experiences and courses taught by real-world professionals. (Classes on various subjects.)

YouTube.com — Our mission is to give everyone a voice and show them the world. (Though it is a social media platform, it includes valuable tutorials about other social media platforms and their features.)

SocialMediaExaminer.com — Our mission is to help you navigate the constantly changing social media jungle. (Though this is aimed at informing people who work in marketing and social media, Social Media Examiner provides tutorials and instructions on all social media platforms and their features.)

Buffer.com/resources — Our vision at Buffer is to build the simplest and most powerful social media tool, and to set the bar for great customer support. (Though Buffer is a tool companies use to manage social media, their company blog provides information and training on social media platforms and their features.)

We believe you can learn technology and social media — but do you believe that? Just like you wouldn't drop off your child at a new school without taking a tour and meeting teachers and staff, you shouldn't drop off your child in the middle of a social media minefield by handing them a miniature supercomputer that they'll only sometimes use as a phone.

Staying ignorant isn't okay. Tell yourself: "I can learn technology and social media." Begin to believe that you can learn these new things well enough to navigate them with your child. We believe in the potential of every parent.

CHAPTER 19

THE DATA

You've heard some of our stories, and you've seen on TV or heard about how a friend's child got caught up in something dangerous online. Stories are emotional. They can scare, inflame, worry, and shock those who hear them. And sometimes, stories that we hear second-hand can be reasoned away or dismissed. However, when the emotion in stories is backed by the hard evidence of numbers, it makes for a far more compelling argument on the side of monitoring your child's usage of technology and social media. We can make rash decisions when we're emotional, and they may not be the best decisions. Be informed and educate yourself on the data.

Here's a sobering look at what we've seen at Bark:

2019 Bark data

In 2019, Bark analyzed more than 874 million messages across texts, email, YouTube, and 30+ apps and social media platforms. These findings exclude school-based accounts.

This data can give parents and guardians important insights into what it's like to grow up on the internet today, allowing them to better protect their children while they use technology.

Cyberbullying

76% of tweens and 78% of teens experienced cyberbullying as a bully, victim or witness.

Alerts for cyberbullying range from mean-spirited teasing to hateful threats and provocations.

Additional external cyberbullying statistics:
- Only 11% of teens[21] talk to parents about incidents of cyberbullying.
- 50% of young gamers[22] experience cyberbullying while playing online.

Mental Health

55% of tweens and 67% of teens engaged in conversations about depression.

Alerts for mental health range from mild pessimism to talking about or planning to attempt suicide.

More national data about mental health:
- 17% of kids[23] ages 6-17 experience a mental health disorder at some point during childhood.
- Major depression increased by 52%[24] among young people between 2005 and 2017.

---

21   http://archive.ncpc.org/resources/files/pdf/bullying/cyberbullying.pdf

22   https://www.bbc.com/news/technology-40092541

23   https://www.nami.org/NAMI/media/NAMI-Media/Infographics/NAMI-You-Are-Not-Alone-FINAL.pdf

24   https://health.usnews.com/wellness/for-parents/articles/2019-04-22/teen-depression-is-on-the-rise

Violence

87% of tweens and 90% of teens expressed or experienced violent subject matter/thoughts.

Alerts for violence range from texting a friend about a fight at school to direct threats against a child.

Relevant U.S. school shooting statistics:
- In 2019, there were 27 gun-related fatalities[25] at schools.
- There were 111 shooting incidents[26] at schools in 2019 — an average of more than two per week.

Drugs/Alcohol

76% of tweens and 85% of teens engaged in conversations surrounding drugs/alcohol.

Alerts for drugs and alcohol can range from texts about prescriptions to videos of a child consuming illegal substances.

General drug/alcohol facts affecting kids today:
- Vaping is on the rise[27] among kids, and teens are now more likely to use e-cigarettes[28] than traditional cigarettes.
- Nicotine exposure can harm adolescent brain development.[29]

25   https://www.chds.us/ssdb/number-killed-by-year/

26   https://www.chds.us/ssdb/incidents-by-year/

27   https://www.fda.gov/tobacco-products/youth-and-tobacco/2018-nyts-data-startling-rise-youth-e-cigarette-use

28   https://www.drugabuse.gov/related-topics/trends-statistics/infographics/teens-e-cigarettes

29   https://www.cdc.gov/tobacco/basic_information/e-cigarettes/about-e-cigarettes.html

Self-Harm/Suicide

35% of tweens and 54% of teens were involved in a self-harm/suicidal situation.

Alerts for potential self-harm and suicide include anything from essays about cutting to an email draft of a suicide note.

National statistics surrounding self-harm/suicide:
- Suicide is the second-leading cause of death[30] for ages 10-24.
- 1 in 10 high school girls[31] will attempt suicide.

Sexual Content

71% of tweens and 84% of teens encountered nudity or content of a sexual nature.

Alerts for sexual content can be anything from references in anatomy and biology homework to a child receiving nude photos.

Recent information regarding kids and sexual content:
- 1 in 4 teens[32] is sexting.
- Sexting laws vary from state to state. Be sure to know the laws[33] in your area.

---

30   https://www.nimh.nih.gov/health/statistics/suicide.shtml

31   https://www.bark.us/beyondthescreen

32   https://time.com/5172906/sexting-messages-teens/

33   https://www.bark.us/blog/state-by-state-differences-in-sexting-laws/

What's your plan?

Now that you've seen the numbers and know the stories, what's your plan of action? What do you need to do in your home to ensure the safety of your children as they navigate the complicated waters of technology and social media?

As we mentioned in the very first chapter, as parents, we must keep the end goal in mind. It's imperative that we have a vision for our children and who we want them to be as adults, and we have to keep trying, day in and day out, to get them there. Don't wait any longer, create an action plan today — the conversations you need to have, the apps or services you need for monitoring, and the limits and agreements you need to set in your home.

CHAPTER 20

CONCLUSION

Empower your relationships to control technology

The very nature of technology is to advance. The tech we have today was built on foundational pillars set in place in the mid-1900s. Every year, humans use technology in increasing ways to improve their lives. Because of this, technology has become an inescapable part of our lives.

But in spite of the proliferation of technology, you can continue to build great relationships with your family members and allow those relationships to guide your use of technology instead of allowing it to control your relationships.

Relationships influence everything we do, and relationships are part of how we understand and interact with the world. The solutions to the problems we face in our technology-driven world aren't chiefly technical. In large part, they're relational. Even the technical solutions we've discussed aren't solutions that will work on their own without strong relationships.

Remember

We control technology through relationships. Relationships are built with conversations.

Conversations start with questions like:

- What have you seen lately that...?
- What's the craziest thing...?
- Can you teach me how...?

You are the parent

Remember who you are. You're the parent. You can be a friend, but you aren't a peer or buddy. Guide your children and teach them how to navigate their lives. Helping them learn how to understand the world of technology can be intimidating. It is an ever-changing landscape of hardware, software, and new devices. But, no matter what new technology comes out between now and the time your children leave your home, the answer to how to guide your family through it is the same. It's about your relationship.

And you can do it!

- You can start asking the right questions to investigate how new technology will affect your family.
- You can find out both what new technology will do *for* you and what it will simply *do*.
- You can ask important questions regularly to deepen your relationship with your family.
- You can set limits and boundaries for the technology in your home in order to make the focus in your home is on relationships and not technology.
- You can learn how to properly use technology in your own life so that you can model for your children how to behave with a phone just as you might model for them how to behave at a fancy dinner party.
- You can control the access points and build trust and responsibility by

checking up on your children as they learn how to use new technology and demonstrate that knowledge.

- You can be on the lookout for behavior that tips you off to problems that could be occurring in your child's world.

Finally, you can cheer your children on as they reach maturity and leave your home, knowing that they can master the use of technology and social media in their lives, and that they won't let technology master them.

AUTHOR BIOGRAPHY

Titania Jordan

Titania Jordan is the CMO and Chief Parent Officer of Bark Technologies.

As the current host of *Tech Connect,* and former host of NBC Atlanta affiliate WXIA's weekly television show *Atlanta Tech Edge,* Titania has the honor of covering the latest in tech news and talent across both the city and the globe.

Titania enjoys helping startups launch in Atlanta by volunteering as a mentor at both Techstars and the Atlanta Tech Village. She travels the country serving as a tech expert on programs such as TODAY Show, Steve Harvey, The Doctors, CBS This Morning, Good Morning America, Fox News, Sirius XM Radio, and CNBC, speaking at esteemed conferences such as VentureBeat MobileBeat, contributing to WSJ, Forbes, Huffington Post, Fox Business, Daily Mail, USA Today, and Vogue, and speaking to groups large and small about the intersection of parenting and tech.

One of her favorite childhood memories is her dad asking her to "figure this new computer thing out" (i.e., read the Microsoft Windows 3.0 user manual) in the early 90s and later teaching him to navigate the wild west of the early internet that would eventually turn into the online world we know today.

AUTHOR BIOGRAPHY

Matt McKee

Matt lives in the Atlanta area with his wife, Jessica, and their two sons, Patriot and Azlan. He likes to say that he's just another guy trying to make a difference.

Matt is an entrepreneur. He has started or helped to start companies for many years. He has failed more times than he has succeeded, but he believes that is the story of most entrepreneurs. Sharing his creativity with others is his passion. He enjoys business conversations over breakfast or lunch more than over a phone call or an email.

For now, Matt uses a MacBook, an iPhone, and an iPad Pro. Since technology is always growing, these devices will soon be traded in for something newer. However, he doesn't plan on leaving the Apple family anytime soon.

CPSIA information can be obtained
at www.ICGtesting.com
Printed in the USA
LVHW092155021120
670541LV00023B/348/J